THE ENDING OF TIME

THE ENDING OF TIME

J. Krishnamurti
& David Bohm

HarperSanFrancisco

A Division of HarperCollinsPublishers

FIRST HARPER & ROW PAPERBACK EDITION PUBLISHED IN 1985

Library of Congress Cataloging in Publication Data

Krishnamurti, J. (Jiddu), 1895–
    The ending of time.

    1. Conflict (Psychology).   2. Time—Psychological aspects.
3. Ego (Psychology).   4. Insight.   5. Thought and thinking.
6. Cosmology.   I. Bohm, David.   II. Title.
BF503.K73   1985   150   84-48773
ISBN 0-06-064796-5 (pbk.)

93 94 95 CWI 16 15 14 13 12 11 10

This book has been prepared from Dialogues that took place between J. Krishnamurti and Professor David Bohm in America and in England between April and September, 1980. On certain occasions other people were present, and their occasional contributions to the discussions, unless otherwise stated, are attributed to 'Questioner' rather than to individuals by name.

CONTENTS

ONE

The Roots of Psychological Conflict

KRISHNAMURTI: How shall we start? I would like to ask if humanity has taken a wrong turn.

DAVID BOHM: A wrong turn? Well it must have done so, a long time ago, I think.

K: That is what I feel. A long time ago . . . It appears that way — why? You see, as I look at it, mankind has always tried to *become* something.

DB: Well possibly. I was struck by something I once read about man going wrong about five or six thousand years ago, when he began to be able to plunder and take slaves. After that, his main purpose of existence was just to exploit and plunder.

K: Yes, but there is the sense of *inward* becoming.

DB: Well, we should make it clear how this is connected. What kind of becoming was involved in doing that? Instead of being constructive, and discovering new techniques and tools and so on, man at a certain time found it easier to plunder his neighbours. Now what did they want to become?

K: Conflict has been the root of all this.

DB: What was the conflict? If we could put ourselves in the place of those people of long ago, how would you see that conflict?

K: What is the root of conflict? Not only outwardly, but also this tremendous inward conflict of humanity? What is the root of it?

DB: Well, it seems that it is contradictory desires.

K: No. Is it that in all religions, you must become something? You must reach something?

DB: Then what made people want to do that? Why weren't they satisfied to be whatever they were? You see, the religion would not have caught on unless people felt that there was some attraction in becoming something more.

K: Isn't it an avoidance, not being able to face the fact, and therefore moving to something else — to more and more and more?

DB: What would you say was the fact that people couldn't stay with?

K: The Christians have said, Original Sin.

DB: But the wrong turn happened long before that.

K: Yes, long before that. Long before that, the Hindus had this idea of Karma. What is the origin of all this?

DB: We have said that there was the fact that people couldn't stay with. Whatever it was, they wanted to imagine something better.

K: Yes, something better. Becoming.

DB: And you could say that they began to make things technologically better, then they extended this, and said, 'I too must become better.'

K: Yes, inwardly become better.

DB: All of us together must become better.

K: That's right. What is the root of all this?

DB: Well, I should think it is natural in thought to project this goal of becoming better. That is, it is intrinsic in the structure of thought.

K: Is it that the principle of becoming better outwardly has moved to becoming better inwardly?

DB: If it is good to become better outwardly, then why shouldn't I become better inwardly?

K: Is that the cause of the conflict?

DB: That is getting towards it. It's coming nearer.

K: Is it coming nearer? Is time the factor? Time — as 'I need knowledge in order to do this or that'? The same principle applied inwardly? Is time the factor?

DB: I can't see that time by itself can be the only factor.

K: No, no. Time. Becoming — which implies time.

DB: Yes, but we don't see how time is going to cause trouble. We have to say that time applied outwardly doesn't cause any difficulty.

K: It causes a certain amount — but we are discussing the idea of time, inwardly.

DB: So we have to see why time is so destructive inwardly.

K: Because I am trying to become something.

DB: Yes, but most people would say that this is only natural. You have to explain what it is that is wrong about becoming.

K: Obviously, there is conflict, in that when I am trying to become something, it is a constant battle.

DB: Yes. Can we go into that: why is it a constant battle? It is not a battle if I try to improve my position outwardly.

K: Outwardly, no. It is more or less all right outwardly, but when that same principle is applied inwardly it brings about a contradiction.

DB: And the contradiction is. . . ?

K: Between 'what is' and 'becoming what should be'.

DB: The difficulty is, why is it a contradiction inwardly and not outwardly?

K: Inwardly it builds up a centre, doesn't it, an egotistic centre?

DB: Yes, but can we find some reason why it should do so? Does it build up when we do it outwardly? It seems it need not.

K: It need not.

DB: But when we are doing it inwardly, then we are trying to force ourselves to be something that we are not.

K: Yes. That is a fact. Is it that one's brain is so accustomed to conflict that one rejects any other form of living?

DB: But why have people come to the conclusion that conflict is inevitable and necessary?

K: What is the origin of conflict?

DB: I think we touched on that by saying that we are trying to force ourselves. When we are a certain thing that we want to be, we also want to be something else, which is different; and therefore we want two different things at the same time. Would that seem right?

K: I understand that. But I am trying to find out the origin of all this misery, confusion, conflict, struggle — what is the beginning of it? That's why I asked at the beginning: has mankind taken a wrong turn? Is the origin, 'I am not I' . . . ?

DB: I think that is getting closer.

K: Yes, that's it. And the 'I' — why has mankind created this 'I', which must, inevitably, cause conflict? 'I' and 'you', and 'I' better than 'you', and so on, and so on.

DB: I think it was a mistake made a long time ago, or, as you call it, a wrong turn, that having introduced separation between various things outwardly, we then kept on doing it — not out of ill will but simply through not knowing better.

K: Quite.

DB: Not seeing what we were doing.

K: Is that the origin of all this conflict?

DB: I am not sure that it is the origin. What do you feel?

K: I am inclined to observe that the origin is the ego, the 'me', the 'I'.

DB: Yes.

K: If there is no ego, there is no problem, there is no conflict, there is no time — time in the sense of becoming or not becoming; being or not being.

DB: But it might be that we would still slip into whatever it was that made us make the ego in the first place.

K: Wait a minute. Is it that energy — being so vast, limitless — has been condensed or narrowed down in the mind, and the brain itself has become narrowed because it couldn't contain all this enormous energy? You are following what I am saying?

DB: Yes.

K: And therefore the brain has gradually narrowed down to 'me', to the 'I'.

DB: I don't quite follow that. I understand that that is what happened, but I don't quite see all the steps. You say energy was enormous and the brain couldn't handle it, or decided that it couldn't handle it?

K: It couldn't handle it.

DB: But if it can't handle it, it seems as if there is no way out.

K: No, just a minute. Go slowly. I just want to enquire, push into it a little bit. Why has the brain, with all thought, created this sense of 'me', 'I'? Why?

DB: We needed a certain sense of identity to function.

K: Yes, to function.

DB: To know where we belong.

K: Yes. And is that the movement which has brought the 'me'? The movement of the outer? I had to identify, with the family, the house, the trade or profession. All this gradually became the 'me'?

DB: I think that this energy that you are talking about also entered into it.

K: Yes, but I want to lead up to that slowly.

DB: You see, what you say is right, that in some way this sense of the 'me' gradually strengthened, but by itself that wouldn't explain the tremendous strength that the ego has. It would only be a habit then. The ego becoming completely dominant required that it should become the focus of the greatest energy; of all the energy.

K: Is that it? That the brain cannot hold this vast energy?

DB: Let's say that the brain is trying to control this — to bring it to order.

K: Energy has no order.

DB: But if the brain feels it can't control something that is going on inside, it will try to establish order.

K: Could we say that the brain, your brain, his brain, her brain, has not just been born; it is very, very old?

DB: In what sense?

K: In the sense that it has evolved.

DB: Evolved, yes, from the animal. And the animal has evolved. So let's say that in a sense this whole evolution is somehow contained in the brain.

K: I want to question evolution. I understand, say, evolution from the bullock cart to the jet.

DB: Yes. But before you question, we have to consider the evidence of man developing through a series of stages. You can't question that, can you?

K: No, of course not.

DB: I mean, physically it is clear that evolution has occurred in some way.

K: Physically, yes.

DB: And the brain has got larger, more complex. But you may question whether mentally evolution has any meaning.

K: You see, I want to abolish time, psychologically. You understand?

DB: Yes, I understand.

K: To me that is the enemy. And is that the cause, the origin of man's misery?

DB: This use of time, certainly. Man had to use time for a certain purpose, but he misused it.

K: I understand that. If I have to learn a language, I must have time.

DB: But the misuse of time by extending it inwardly . . .

K: *Inwardly*: that is what I am talking about. Is that the cause of man's confusion — introducing time as a means of becoming, and becoming more and more perfect, more and more evolved, more and more loving? You follow what I mean?

DB: Yes, I understand. Certainly if we didn't do that, the whole structure would collapse.

K: That's it.

DB: But I don't know whether there is not some other cause.

K: Just a minute. I want to go into that a little bit. I am not talking theoretically, personally. But to me the idea of tomorrow doesn't exist psychologically — that is, time as a movement, either inwardly or outwardly.

DB: You mean psychological time?

K: Yes, psychological time, and time outwardly. Now if psychological time doesn't exist, then there is no conflict, there is no 'me', no 'I', which is the origin of conflict. Outwardly, technologically man has moved, evolved.

DB: And also in the inward physical structure.

K: The structure, everything. But psychologically we have also moved outward.

DB: Yes, we have focused our life on the outward. Is that what you are saying?

K: Yes. We have extended our capacities outwardly. And inwardly it is the same movement as outwardly. Now if there is no inward movement as time, moving, becoming more and more, then what takes place? You understand what I am trying to convey? Time ends. You see, the outer movement is the same as the inward movement.

DB: Yes. It is going around and around.

K: Involving time. If the movement ceases, then what takes place? I wonder if I am conveying anything? Could we put it this way? We have never touched any other movement than the outer movement.

DB: Generally, anyway. We put most of our energy into the outer movements.

K: And psychological movement is also outward.

DB: Well, it is the reflection of that outward movement.

K: We think it is inward but it is actually outward, right?

DB: Yes.

K: Now if that movement ends, as it must, then is there a really inward movement — a movement not in terms of time?

DB: You are asking, is there another kind of movement which still moves, but not in terms of time?

K: That's right.

DB: We have to go into that. Could you go further?

K: You see, that word movement means time.

DB: Well, it really means to change from one place to another. But anyway there is still the notion of something which is not static. By denying time you don't want to return to something static, which is still time.

K: Let's say, for instance, that one's brain has been trained, accustomed, for centuries to go North. And it suddenly realizes that going North means everlasting conflict. As it realizes that, the brain itself changes — the quality of the brain changes.

DB: All right. I can see it will wake up in some way to a different movement.

K: Yes, different.

DB: Is the word flow any better?

K: I have been going North all my life, and there is a sudden stoppage from going North. But the brain is not going East or South or West. Then conflict ceases — right? Because it is not moving in any direction.

DB: So that is the key point — the direction of movement. When the movement is fixed in direction, inwardly, it will come to conflict. But outwardly we need a fixed direction.

K: Of course we do. That's understood.

DB: Yes. So if we say the brain has no fixed direction, then what is it doing? Is it moving in all directions?

K: I am a little bit hesitant to talk about this. Could one say, when one really comes to that state, that it is the source of all energy?

DB: Yes, as one goes deeper and more inward.

K: This is the real inwardness; not the outward movement becoming the inner movement, but no outer or inner movement . . .

DB: Yes, we can deny both the outward and the inner, so that all movement would seem to stop.

K: Would that be the source of all energy?

DB: Yes, perhaps we could say that.

K: May I talk about myself a little bit?

DB: Yes.

K: First about meditation. All conscious meditation is no meditation — right?

DB: What do you mean by conscious meditation?

K: Deliberate, practised meditation, which is really pre-meditated meditation. Is there a meditation which is not premeditated — which is not the ego trying to become something — or being able to negate?

DB: Before we go ahead, could we suggest what meditation should be. Is it an observation of the mind observing? .

K: No. It has gone beyond all that. I am using the word meditation in the sense in which there is not a particle of any sense of trying consciously to become, to reach a level.

DB: The mind is simply with itself, silent.

K: That is what I want to get at.

DB: Not looking for anything.

K: You see, I don't meditate in the normal sense of the word. What happens is that I wake up meditating.

DB: In that state?

K: One night in India I woke up; it was a quarter past twelve, I looked at the watch. And — I hesitate to say this because it sounds extravagant — the source of all energy had been reached. And that had an extraordinary effect on the brain. And also physically. I'm sorry to talk about myself, but, you understand, literally, there was no division at all; no sense of the world, of 'me'. You follow? Only this sense of a tremendous source of energy.

DB: So the brain was in contact with this source of energy?

K: Yes, and as I have been talking for sixty years, I would like others to reach this — no, not *reach* it. You understand what I am saying? All our problems are solved. Because it is pure energy from the very beginning of time. Now how am I — not 'I', you understand — how is one not to teach, not to help, or push — but how is one to say, 'This way leads to a complete sense of peace, of love'? I am sorry to use all these words. But suppose you have come to that point and your brain itself is throbbing with it — how would you help another? You understand? Help — not words. How would you help another to come to that? You understand what I am trying to say?

DB: Yes.

K: My brain — but not mine — has evolved. Evolution implies time, and it can only think, live in time. Now for the brain to deny time is a tremendous activity, for any problem that arises, any question is immediately solved.

DB: Is this situation sustained or is it only for a period?

K: It is sustained, obviously, otherwise there is no point in it. It is not sporadic or intermittent. Now how are you to open the door, how are you to help another to say, 'Look, we have been going in the wrong direction, there is only non-movement; and, if movement stops, everything will be correct'?

DB: Well, it is hard to know beforehand if everything is going to be correct.

K: Let's go back to what we began with. That is, has mankind taken a wrong turn, psychologically, not physically? Can that turn be completely reversed? Or stopped? My brain is so accustomed to this evolutionary idea that I will become something, I will gain something, that I must have more knowledge and so on; can that brain suddenly realize that there is no such thing as time? You understand what I am trying to say?

DB: Yes.

K: I was listening the other day to a discussion on television about Darwin, his knowledge and what he achieved — his whole theory of evolution. It seems to me that this is totally untrue psychologically.

DB: It seems that he has given evidence that all species have changed in time. Why is that untrue?

K: Of course. It is obvious.

DB: It is true in one respect, although I think it would be untrue to say the mind evolved in time.

K: Of course.

DB: But *physically* it seems clear there has been a process of evolution, and that this has increased the capacity of the brain to do certain things. For example, we couldn't be discussing this if the brain had not grown larger.

K: Of course.

DB: But I think you are implying that the mind is not originating in the brain. Is that so? The brain is perhaps an instrument of the mind?

K: And the mind is not time. Just see what that means.

DB: The mind does not evolve with the brain.

K: The mind not being of time, and the brain being of time — is that the origin of conflict?

DB: Well, we have to see why that produces conflict. It is not clear to say that the brain is of time, but rather that it has developed in such a way that time is in it.

K: Yes, that is what I meant.

DB: But not necessarily so.

K: It has evolved.

DB: It has evolved, so it has time within it.

K: Yes, it has evolved, time is part of it.

DB: It has become part of its very structure.

K: Yes.

DB: However, the mind operates without time, although the brain is not able to do so.

K: That means that God is in man, and God can only operate if the brain is quiet, if the brain is not caught in time.

DB: Well, I wasn't meaning that. I see that the brain, having a structure of time, is not able to respond properly to mind. That's really what seems to be involved here.

K: Can the brain itself see that it is caught in time, and that as long as it is moving in that direction, conflict is eternal, endless? You follow what I am saying?

DB: Yes. Does the brain see it?

K: Has the brain the capacity to see in what it is doing now — being caught in time — that in that process there is no end to conflict? That means, is there a part of the brain which is not of time?

DB: Not caught or functioning in time?

K: Can one say that?

DB: I don't know.

K: That would mean — we come back to the same thing in different words — that the brain is not being completely conditioned by time, so there is a part of the brain that is free of time.

DB: Not a part, but rather that the brain is mainly dominated by time, although that doesn't necessarily mean it couldn't shift.

K: Yes. That is, can the brain, dominated by time, not be subservient to it?

DB: That's right. In that moment it comes out of time. I think I can see this — it is dominated only when you give it time. Thought which takes time is dominated, but anything fast enough is not dominated.

K: Yes, that's right. Can the brain — which has been used to time — can it see in that process that there is no end to conflict? See, in the sense of realizing this? Will it realize it under pressure? Certainly not. Will it realize it under coercion, reward or punishment? It will not. It will either resist or escape.

So what is the factor that will make the brain see that the way it has been functioning is not correct? (Let's use that word for the moment.) And what will make it suddenly realize that it is totally mischievous? What will make it? Certainly not drugs or some kind of chemical.

DB: None of these outward things.

K: Then what will make the brain realize this?

DB: What do you mean by realize?

K: Realize that the path along which the brain has been going will always be the path of conflict.

DB: I think this raises the question that the brain resists such a realization.

K: Of course, of course. Because it has been used to the old path, for centuries! How will you make the brain realize this fact? If you could make it realize that, conflict is finished.

You see, people have tried fasting, austerity, poverty, chastity in the real sense, purity, having a mind that is absolutely correct; they have tried going away by themselves; they have tried practically everything that man has invented, but none of these ways has succeeded.

DB: Well, what do *you* say? It is clear that people pursuing these outward goals are still becoming.

K: Yes, but they never realize that these are outward goals. It means denying all that completely.

DB: You see, to go further, I think that one has to deny the very notion of time in the sense of looking forward to the future, and deny all the past.

K: That's just it.

DB: That is, the whole of time.

K: Time is the enemy. Meet it, and go beyond it.

DB: Deny that it has an independent existence. You see, I think we have the impression that time exists independently of us. We are in the stream of time, and therefore it would seem absurd for us to deny it because that is what we are.

K: Yes, quite, quite. So it means *really* moving away — again this is only words — from *everything* that man has put together as a means of timelessness.

DB: Can we say that none of the methods that man uses outwardly is going to free the mind from time?

K: Absolutely.

DB: Every method implies time.

K: Of course. It is so simple.

DB: We start out immediately by setting up the whole structure of time; the whole notion of time is presupposed before we start.

K: Yes, quite. But how will you convey this to another? How will you, or 'X', convey this to a man who is caught in time and will resist it, fight it, because he says there is no other way? How will you convey this to him?

DB: I think that you can only convey it to somebody who has gone into it; you are not likely to convey it at all to somebody you just pick up off the street!

K: So then, what are we doing? As that cannot be conveyed through words, what is a man to do? Would you say that to resolve a problem as it arises you have to go into it immediately, because otherwise you may do the most foolish thing and delude yourself that you have resolved it? Suppose I have a problem, any psychological problem — can the mind realize, resolve it immediately? Not deceive itself, not resist it — you understand? But face it, and end it.

DB: Well, with a psychological problem, that is the only way. Otherwise we would be caught in the very source of the problem.

K: Of course. Would that activity end time, the psychological time that we are talking about?

DB: Yes, if we could bring this immediate action to bear on the problem, which is the self.

K: One is greedy, or envious. *To end immediately* greed, attachment, and so on, will that not give a clue to the ending of time?

DB: Yes, because any action which is not immediate has already brought in time.

K: Yes, yes. I know that.

DB: The ending of time is immediate — right?

K: Immediate, of course. Would that point out the wrong turn that mankind has taken?

DB: Yes, if man feels something is out of order psychologically he then brings in the notion of time, and the thought of becoming, and that creates endless problems.

K: Would that open the door to this sense of time having no place inwardly? Which means, doesn't it, that thought has no place except outwardly?

DB: You are saying that thought is a process which is involved in time.

K: Wouldn't you say that thought is the process of time? Because thought is based on experience, knowledge, memory and response, which is the whole of time.

DB: Let's try to put it that thought, as we have generally known it, is in time.

K: Thought as we know it now is of time.

DB: Yes. I would agree, generally speaking.

K: Generally speaking, thought is time.

DB: It is based on the notion of time.

K: Yes, all right. But to me, thought itself is time.

DB: Thought itself creates time, right.

K: Does it mean, when there is no time there is no thought?

DB: Well, no thought of that kind.

K: No. There is *no* thought. I want just to go slowly.

DB: Could we say that there is a kind of thought which we have lived in which has been dominated by time?

K: Yes, but that has come to an end.

DB: But there may be another kind of thought which is not dominated by time. . . . I mean, you were saying, you could still use thought to do some things.

K: Of course, outwardly that's so.

DB: We have to be careful not to say that thought is necessarily dominated by time.

K: Yes. I have to go from here to there, to my house; that needs time, thought, but I am not talking of that kind of time.

DB: So let's make it clear that you are talking of thought which is aimed at the mind, whose content is the order of the mind.

K: Yes. Would you say knowledge is time?

DB: Well, yes . . .

K: All knowledge is time.

DB: Yes, in that it has been known, and may project into the future, and so on.

K: Of course, the future, the past. Knowledge — science, mathematics, whatever it is — is acquired through time. I read philosophy, I read this or that, and the whole movement of knowledge involves time. See what I mean!

DB: I think we are saying that man has taken a wrong turn and got caught in this kind of knowledge, which is dominated by time because it has become psychological knowledge.

K: Yes. So he lives in time.

DB: He lives in time because he has attempted to produce knowledge of the nature of the mind. Are you saying that there is no real knowledge of the mind? Would you put it that way?

K: The moment you use the word 'knowledge', it implies time. When you end time, in the sense we are talking about, there is no knowledge as experience.

DB: We have to see what the word 'experience' means.

K: Experience, memory.

DB: People say, 'I learn by experience, I go through something.'

K: Which is becoming!

DB: Well, let's get it clear. You see there is a kind of experience, for example, in one's job, which becomes skill and perception.

K: Of course, but that is quite different.

DB: But we are saying there is no point in having experience of the mind, psychological experience.

K: Yes, let's put it that way. Psychological experience is in time.

DB: Yes, and it has no point, because you cannot say, 'As I become skilled in my job I will become skilled in my mind, or skilled fundamentally'.

K: Yes. So where is this leading? I realize that knowledge is time; the brain realizes it, and sees the importance of time in a certain direction, and that there is no value in time at all in another direction. It is not a contradiction.

DB: I would put it that the value of time is limited to a certain direction or area, and beyond that, it has no value.

K: Yes. So what is the mind or the brain without knowledge? You understand.

DB: Without psychological knowledge?

K: Yes, I am talking psychologically.

DB: It is not so much that it is caught in time as that it is without psychological knowledge to organize itself.

K: Yes.

DB: So we are saying that the brain field must organize itself by knowing psychologically all about itself.

K: Is then the mind, the brain, disorder? Certainly not.

DB: No. But I think that people being faced with this might feel there would be disorder.

K: Of course.

DB: I think what you are saying is that the notion of controlling yourself psychologically has no meaning.

K: So knowledge of the 'me' — the psychological knowledge — is time.

DB: Yes, I understand the totality of knowledge is 'me', is time.

K: So then what is existence without this? There is no time, there is no knowledge in the psychological sense, no sense of 'me', then what is there? To come to that point most people would say, 'What a horror this is.'

DB: Yes, because it seems there would be nothing.

K: Nothing. But if one has come to that point, what is there? Would you say, because there is nothing, it is everything?

DB: Yes, I would accept that. I know that. That is true, it has all.

K: No meditation, nothing.

DB: No thing.

K: No thing, that's right.

DB: A thing is limited, and this is not a thing because there are no limits . . . At least, it has everything in potential.

K: Wait, Sir. If it is nothing, and so everything, so everything is energy.

DB: Yes. The ground of everything is energy.

K: Of course. Everything is energy. And what is the source of this thing? Or is there no souce of energy at all? Is there only energy?

DB: Energy just is. Energy is 'what is'. There is no need for a source. That is one approach, perhaps?

K: No. If there is nothing, and therefore everything, and everything is energy . . . We must be very careful because here, the Hindus have this idea too, which is that Brahman is everything. You understand? But that becomes an idea, a principle, and then functioning is once more in the brain. But the fact of it is, there is nothing, therefore there is everything, and all that is cosmic energy. But what started this energy?

DB: We are not talking of time.

K: I know we are not talking of time, but you see the Christians would say, 'God is energy and He is the source of all energy.' No?

DB: But the Christians have an idea of what they call the Godhead, which is the very source of God too.

K: And also the Hindus, the Arabic and the Jewish worlds have this. Are we going against all that?

DB: It sounds similar in some ways.

K: And yet not similar. We must be careful.

DB: Many things like this have been said over the ages.

K: Then is one just walking in emptiness? Is one living in emptiness?

DB: Well, that is not clear.

K: There is nothing, and everything is energy. What is this?

DB: Well, is there something within the energy?

K: This is not different from energy. This. But the thing that is inside says, 'I am totally different from that'.

DB: The 'I' encloses itself and says, 'I am different, I am eternal.'

K: Why has it done this? Why has the separation arisen? Is it because outwardly I identify with a house and so on, and that identification has moved inwardly?

DB: Yes. And the second point was that once we established a notion of something inward, then it became necessary to protect that. And therefore that built up the separation.

K: Of course.

DB: The inward was obviously the most precious thing, and it would have to be protected with all our energy.

K: Does it mean then that there is only the organism — which is part of energy? There is no 'me' at all, except the passport name and form; otherwise nothing. And therefore there is everything, and therefore all is energy?

DB: Yes, the form has no independent existence.

K: No. There is only the form. That's all.

DB: There is also the energy, you say.

K: That is part of energy. So there is only this, the outward shape.

DB: There is the outward form in the energy.

K: Do you realize what we have said, Sir? Is this the end of the journey?

DB: No, I should think not.

K: Has mankind journeyed through millenia to come to this? That I am nothing, and therefore I am everything, and all energy.

DB: Well it can't be the end, in the sense that it might be the beginning.

K: Wait. That is all I wanted you to begin with. The ending is the beginning — right? Now I want to go into that. You see, in the ending of all this — the ending of time, we will call it briefly — there is a new beginning. What is that? Because otherwise this seems so utterly futile. I am all energy and just the shell exists, and time has ended. It seems so futile.

DB: Yes, if we stop there. . . .

K: That's all.

DB: I think that really this is clearing the ground of all the debris, of all the confusion.

K: Yes. So the ending is a beginning. But what is that? Beginning implies time also.

DB: Not necessarily. I think we said there could be a movement which had no time.

K: That is all. I want to make it clear.

DB: Yes, but it is hard to express. It is not a question of being static, but in some sense the movement has not the order of time. I think we would have to say that now.

K: Yes. So we will use the word 'beginning' and deprive it of time.

DB: Because ending and beginning are no special time. In fact they can be any time or no time.

K: No time. Then what takes place? What is happening? Not to me, not to my brain. What is happening? We have said that when one denies time there is nothing. After this long talk, nothing means everything. Everything is energy. And we have stopped there. But that isn't the end.

DB: No.

K: That is not the end. Then what is going on? Is that creation?

DB: Yes, something like that.

K: But not the art of creating like writing or painting.

DB: Perhaps later we can discuss what we mean by creating.

1 APRIL 1980, OJAI, CALIFORNIA

TWO

Cleansing the Mind of the Accumulation of Time

KRISHNAMURTI: We were saying that psychological time is conflict, that time is the enemy of man. And that enemy has existed from the beginning of man. And we asked, why has man from the beginning taken a 'wrong turn', a 'wrong path'? And, if so, is it possible to turn man in another direction in which he can live without conflict? Because, as we said yesterday, the outer movement is also the same as the inner movement. There is no separation between inner and outer. It is the same movement. And we asked whether we were concerned deeply and passionately to turn man in another direction so that he doesn't live in time, with a knowledge only of the outer things. The religions, the politicians, the educators have failed: they have never been concerned about this. Would you agree to that?

DAVID BOHM: Yes. I think the religions have tried to discuss the eternal values beyond time but they don't seem to have succeeded.

K: That is what I want to get at. To them it has been an idea, an ideal, a principle, a value, but not an actuality, and most of the religious people have their anchor in a belief, in a principle, in an image, in knowledge, in Jesus or in something or other.

DB: Yes, but if you were to consider all the religions, say the various forms of Buddhism, they try to say this very thing which you are saying, to some extent.

K: To some extent but what I am trying to get at is: why has man never confronted this problem? Why haven't we said 'Let's end conflict'? Instead we have been encouraged because through conflict we think there is progress.

DB: It can be a certain source of stimulus to try to overcome opposition.

K: Yes, Sir, but if you and I see the truth of this, not in abstraction, but actually, deeply, can we act in such a way that every issue is resolved instantly, immediately, so that psychological time is abolished? And as we asked yesterday, when you come to that point where there is nothing and there is everything, where all that is energy — when time ends, is there a beginning of something totally new? Is there a beginning which is not enmeshed in time? Now how shall we discover it? Words are necessary to communicate. But the word is not that thing. So what is there when all time ends? Psychological time, not time of . . .

DB: . . . time of day.

K: Yes. Time as the 'me', the ego, and when that completely comes to an end, what is there that begins? Could we say that out of the ashes of time there is a new growth? What is that which begins — no, that word 'begins' implies time too.

DB: Whatever we mean, that which arises.

K: That arises, what is it?

DB: Well, as we said yesterday, essentially it is creation, the possibility of creation.

K: Yes, creation. Is that it? Is something new being born?

DB: It is not the process of becoming.

K: Oh, no, that is finished. Becoming is the worst, that is time, that is the real root of this conflict. We are trying to find out what happens when the 'I', which is time, has completely come to an end. I believe the Buddha is supposed to have said 'Nirvana'. And the Hindus call it Moksha. I don't know whether the Christians call it Heaven . . .

DB: The Christian mystics have had some similar state . . .

K: Similar, yes. But you see, the Christian mystics, as far as I understand it, are rooted in Jesus, in the Church, in the whole belief. They have never gone beyond it.

DB: Yes, well that seems so. As far as I know anyway.

K: Now we have said belief, attachment to all that is out, finished. That is all part of the 'I'. Now when there is that absolute cleansing of the mind from the accumulation of time, which is the essence of the 'me', what takes place? Why should we ask what takes place?

DB: You mean it is not a good question?

K: I am just asking myself, why should we ask that? Is there behind it a subtle form of hope? A subtle form of saying, I have reached that point, there is nothing. Then that's a wrong question. Wouldn't you consider that so?

DB: Well, it invites you to look for some hopeful outcome.

K: If all endeavour is to find something beyond the 'me', that endeavour and the thing that I may find are still within the orbit of 'me'. So I have no hope. There is no sense of hope, there is no sense of wanting to find anything.

DB: What is then moving you to enquire?

K: My enquiry has been to end conflict.

DB: Yes, we have then to be careful. We are liable to produce a hope of ending conflict.

K: No, no; there is no hope. I end it. The moment I introduce the word 'hope' there is a feeling of the future.

DB: Yes, that is desire.

K: Desire — and therefore it is of time. So I — the mind — puts all that aside completely; I mean it, completely. Then what is the essence of all this? Is my mind still seeking, or groping after something intangible that it can capture and hold? If that is so, it is still part of time.

DB: Well, that is still desire.

K: Desire and a subtle form of vanity.

DB: Why vanity?

K: Vanity in the sense 'I have reached'.

DB: Self-deception.

K: Deception and all forms of illusion arise from that. So it is not that. I am clearing the decks as we go along.

DB: Essentially it seems that you are clearing the movement of desire in its subtle forms.

K: In its subtle forms. So desire too has been put away. Then there is only mind — right?

DB: Yes, but then we have to ask what is meant by nature, if all is mind, because nature seems somewhat independent.

K: But we have also said that all the universe is the mind.

DB: You mean to say nature is the mind?

K: Part of the mind.

DB: The universal mind?

K: Yes.

DB: Not a particular mind?

K: The particular mind then is separate, but we are talking of Mind.

DB: You see, we have to make it clear, because you are saying that nature is the creation of universal mind, though nevertheless nature has a certain reality.

K: That is all understood.

DB: But it is almost as if nature were the thought of the universal mind.

K: It is part of it. I am trying to grope towards the particular mind coming to an end; then there is only the Mind, the universal mind — right?

DB: Yes. We have been discussing the particular mind groping through desire, and we said if all of that stopped . . .

K: That is just my point. If all that has completely come to an end, what is the next step? *Is* there any next? We said yesterday, there is a beginning, but that word implies part of time.

DB: We won't say so much beginning, perhaps ending.

K: The ending, we have said that.

DB: But now is there something new?

K: Is there something which the mind cannot capture?

DB: Which mind, the particular or the universal?

K: The particular has ended.

DB: Yes. You are saying the universal mind cannot capture it either?

K: That is what we are finding out.

DB: Are you saying there is a reality — or something — beyond universal mind?

K: Are we playing a game of peeling off one thing after another? Like an onion skin, and at the end there is only tears and nothing else?

DB: Well, I don't know.

K: Because we said there is the ending, then the cosmic, the universal mind, and, beyond, is there something more?

DB: Well, would you say this 'more' is energy? That energy is beyond the universal mind?

K: I would say yes, because the universal mind is part of that energy.

DB: That is understandable. In a way the energy is alive, you are saying?

K: Yes, yes.

DB: And also intelligent?

K: Wait a minute.

DB: In some way. . . . In so far as it is mind.

K: Now if that energy is intelligent, why has it allowed man to move away in the wrong direction?

DB: I think that that may be part of a process, something that is inevitable in the nature of thought. You see if thought is going to develop, that possibility must exist. To bring about thought in man. . .

K: Is that the original freedom for man? To choose?

DB: No, that is, thought has to have the capacity to make this mistake.

K: But if that intelligence was operating, why did it allow this mistake?

DB: Well, we can suggest that there is a universal order, a law.

K: All right. The universe functions in order.

DB: Yes, and it is part of the order of the universe that this particular mechanism can go wrong. If a machine breaks down, it is not disorder in the universe, it is part of universal order.

K: Yes. In the universal order there is disorder, where man is concerned.

DB: It is not disorder at the level of the universe.

K: No. At a much lower level.

DB: At the level of man it is disorder.

K: And why has man lived from the beginning in this disorder?

DB: Because he is still ignorant, he still hasn't seen the point.

K: But he is part of the whole, yet in one tiny corner man exists, and has lived in disorder. And this enormous conscious intelligence has not . . .

DB: Yes, you could say that the possibility of creation is also the possibility of disorder. That if man had the possibility of being creative, there would also be the possibility of a mistake. It could not be fixed like a machine, always to operate in perfect order. The intelligence would not have turned him into a machine that would be incapable of disorder.

K: No, of course not. So is there something beyond the cosmic order, mind?

DB: Are you saying that the universe, that that mind, has created nature which has an order, which is not merely going around mechanically? It has some deeper meaning?

K: That is what we are trying to find out.

DB: You are bringing in the whole universe as well as mankind. What makes you do this? What is the source of this perception?

K: Let's begin again: there is the ending of the 'me' as time, and so there is no hope; all that is finished, ended. In the ending of it, there is that sense of nothingness. And nothingness is this whole universe.

DB: Yes, the universal mind, the universal matter.

K: The whole universe.

DB: What led you to say that?

K: Ah. I know. To put it very simply: division has come to an end. Right? The division created by time, created by thought, created by this education, and so on — all that. Because it has ended, the other is obvious.

DB: You mean that without the division then the other is there — to be perceived?

K: Not to be perceived, but it is there.

DB: But then how does one come to be aware that it is there?

K: I don't think one becomes aware of it.

DB: Then what leads you to say it?

K: Would you say it *is*? Not, I perceive it, or it is perceived.

DB: Yes. It is.

K: It is.

DB: You could almost say that *it* is saying it. In some sense, you seem to be suggesting that *it* is what is saying.

K: Yes. I didn't want to put it — I am glad you put it like that! Where are we now?

DB: We are saying that the universe is alive, as it were, it is mind, and we are part of it.

K: We can only say we are part of it when there is no 'I'.

DB: No division.

K: No division. I would like to push it a little further; is there something beyond all this?

DB: Beyond the energy, you mean?

K: Yes. We said nothingness, that nothingness is everything, and so it is that which is total energy. It is undiluted, pure, uncorrupted energy. Is there something beyond that? Why do we ask it?

DB: I don't know.

K: I feel we haven't touched it — I feel there is something beyond.

DB: Could we say this something beyond is the ground of the whole? You are saying that all this emerges from an inward ground?

K: Yes, there is another — I must be awfully careful here. You know one must be awfully careful not to be romantic, not to have illusions, not to have desire, not even to search. It must happen. You follow what I mean?

DB: We are saying the thing must come from *that*. Whatever you are saying must come from that.

K: From that. That's it. It sounds rather presumptuous.

DB: You are actually seeing it. It is not that you look at it and say, that is what I have seen.

K: Oh, no. Then it is wrong.

DB: There isn't a division. Of course, it is easy to fall into delusion with this sort of thing.

K: Yes, but we said delusion exists as long as there is desire and thought. That is simple. And desire and thought are part of the 'I', which is time. When desire and time are completely ended, then there is absolutely nothing, and therefore that is the universe, that emptiness, which is full of energy. We can put a stop there. . . .

DB: Because we haven't yet seen the necessity for going beyond the energy. We have to see that as necessary.

K: I think it is necessary.

DB: Yes, but it has to be seen. We have to bring out why it is necessary.

K: Why is it necessary? Tentatively, there is something in us that is operating, there is something in us much more — much — I don't know how to put it — much greater. I am going slowly, slowly. What I am trying to say is, I think there is something beyond that. When I say 'I think', you know what I mean.

DB: I understand, yes.

K: There is something beyond that. How can we talk about it? You see, energy exists only when there is emptiness. They go together.

DB: This pure energy you talk about is emptiness. Are you suggesting there is that which is beyond the emptiness, the ground of the emptiness?

K: Yes.

DB: Would that be something in the way of a substance? You see the question is, if it is not emptiness, then what is it?

K: I don't quite follow your question.

DB: Well, you say something beyond emptiness, other than emptiness. I think we can follow to the energy and the emptiness. Now if we suggest something other to that, to the emptiness . . .

K: This something other.

DB: Yes, then that other must be different from the emptiness. Something other to emptiness, which therefore is not emptiness. Does that make sense?

K: Then it is substance.

DB: Yes, that is what is implied: if it is not emptiness, it is substance.

K: Substance is matter, is it not?

DB: Not necessarily, but having the quality of substance.

K: What do you mean by that?

DB: Matter is a form of substance in the sense that it is energy, but having the form of substance as well, because it has a constant form and it resists change. It is stable, it maintains itself.

K: Yes. But when you use the word 'substance', meaning beyond emptiness, does that word convey that meaning?

DB: Well, we are exploring the possible meaning of what you want to say. If you are saying it is not emptiness, then it would not be substance as we know it in matter. But we can see a certain quality which belongs to substance in general; if it has that quality, we could use the word substance, extend the meaning of the word substance.

K: I understand. So could we use the word 'quality'?

DB: The word 'quality' is not necessarily the emptiness, energy could have the quality of emptiness, you see. And therefore it is something else. Something other might have the quality of substance. That is the way I see it. And is that what you are trying to say?

K: There is something beyond emptiness. How shall we tackle it?

DB: Firstly, what leads you to say this?

K: Simply the fact that there is. We have been fairly logical all along, we have not been caught in any illusions so far. And can we keep that same kind of watchfulness, in which there is no illusion, to find out — or, not find out — that which is beyond emptiness? To come down to earth. Come down to earth in the sense to be communicated. You follow what I mean?

DB: Yes. Well we could come back to the question before: why hasn't it come down?

K: Why hasn't it come down? Has man been ever free from the 'I'?

DB: No. Not generally speaking.

K: No. And it demands that the 'I' ends.

DB: I think we could look at it this way: that the ego becomes an illusion of that substance. You feel the ego is a substance too in some way.

K: Yes, the ego is substance.

DB: And therefore that substance seems to be . . .

K: . . . untouchable.

DB: But that ego is an illusion of the true substance — it may be that the mind tries to create some sort of illusion of that substance.

K: That is an illusion. Why do you relate it to the other?

DB: In the sense that if the mind thinks it already has this substance, then it will not be open . . .

K: Of course not. Can that thing ever be put into words? It is not a question of avoiding something, or trying to slither out of some conclusion. But you see, so far we have put everything into words.

DB: Well, I think that once something is properly perceived, then after a while the words come to communicate it.

K: Yes, but can *that* be perceived? And therefore be communicable? Is this beyond . . . ?

DB: This thing beyond, would you say also it is alive? Life beyond emptiness, is that still life? Living?

K: Living, yes. Oh, yes.

DB: And intelligent?

K: I don't want to use those words.

DB: They are too limited?

K: Living, intelligence, love, compassion; they are all too limited. You and I are sitting here. We have come to a point and there is that thing which perhaps later on might be put into words without any sense of pressure, and so without any illusion. Don't you see beyond the wall? — the word, I mean? We have come to a certain point, and we are saying there is something still more — you understand? There is something behind all that. Is it palpable? Can we touch it? Is it something that the mind can capture? You follow?

DB: Yes. Are you saying it is not?

K: I don't think it is possible for the mind to capture it . . .

DB: Or grasp it . . . ?

K: Grasp it, understand . . . for the mind even to look at it. You are a scientist, you have examined the atom, and so on. Don't you, when you have examined all that, feel there is something much more, beyond all that?

DB: You can always feel that there is more beyond that, but it doesn't tell you what it is. It is clear that whatever one knows is limited.

K: Yes.

DB: And there must be more beyond.

K: How can that communicate with you, so that you, with your scientific knowledge, with your brain capacity can grasp it?

DB: Are you saying it can't be grasped?

K: No. How can you grasp it? I don't say you can't grasp it. Can you grasp it?

DB: Look, it is not clear. You were saying before that it is ungraspable by . . .

K: Grasp, in the sense, can your mind go beyond theories. . . ? What I am trying to say is, can you move into it? Not move, in the sense of time and all that. Can you enter it? No, those are all words. What is beyond emptiness? Is it silence?

DB: Isn't that similar to emptiness?

K: Yes, that is what I am getting at. Move step by step. Is it silence? Or is silence part of emptiness?

DB: Yes, I should say that.

K: I should say that too. If it is not silence, could we — I am just asking — could we say it is something absolute? You understand?

DB: Well, we could consider the absolute. It would have to be something totally independent; that is what 'absolute' really means. It doesn't depend on anything.

K: Yes. You are getting somewhere near it.

DB: Entirely self moving, as it were, self active.

K: Yes. Would you say everything has a cause, and *that* has no cause at all?

DB: You see, this notion is already an old one. This notion has been developed by Aristotle, that this absolute is the cause of itself.

K: Yes.

DB: It has no cause, in a sense. That is the same thing.

K: You see the moment you said Aristotle . . . it is not that. How shall we get at this? Emptiness is energy, and that emptiness exists in silence, or the other way round, it doesn't matter — right? Oh, yes, there is something beyond all this. Probably it can never be put into words. But it must be put into words. You follow?

DB: You are saying that the absolute must be put into words, but we feel it can't be? Any attempt to put it into words makes it relative.

K: Yes. I don't know how to put all this.

DB: I think that we have a long history of danger with the absolute. People have put it in words, and it has become very oppressive.

K: Leave all that. You see, being ignorant of what other people have said, Aristotle and the Buddha, and so on, has an advantage. You understand what I mean? An advantage in the sense that the mind is not coloured by other people's ideas, not caught in other people's statements. All that is part of our conditioning. Now, to go beyond all that! What are we trying to do?

DB: I think, to communicate regarding this absolute, this beyond.

K: I took away that word 'absolute' immediately.

DB: Then whatever it is; the beyond emptiness and silence.

K: Beyond all that. There is beyond all that. All that is something, part of an immensity.

DB: Yes, well even the emptiness and silence is an immensity, isn't it? The energy is itself an immensity.

K: Yes, I understand that. But there is something much more immense than that. Emptiness and silence and energy are immense, really immeasurable. But there is something — I am using the word, 'greater', than that.

DB: I am just considering. I am looking at it. One can see that whatever you say about emptiness, or about any other thing, there is something beyond.

K: No, as a scientist, why do you accept — not accept, forgive me for using that word — why do you even move along with this?

DB: Because we have come this far step by step, seeing the necessity of each step.

K: You see all that is very logical, reasonable, sane.

DB: And also, one can see that it is so right.

K: Yes. So if I say there is something greater than all this silence, energy — would you accept that? Accept in the sense that up to now we have been logical.

DB: We will say that whatever you speak of there is certainly something beyond it. Silence, energy, whatever, then there is always room logically for something beyond that. But the point is this: that even if you were to say there is something beyond that, still you logically leave room for going again beyond that.

K: No.

DB: Well why is that? You see, whatever you say, there is always room for something beyond.

K: There is nothing beyond.

DB: Well that point is not clear, you see.

K: There is nothing beyond it. I stick to that. Not dogmatically or obstinately. I feel that is the beginning and the ending of everything. The ending and the beginning are the same — right?

DB: In which sense? In the sense that you are using the beginning of everything as the ending?

K: Yes. Right? You would say that?

DB: Yes. If we take the ground from which it comes, it must be the ground to which it falls.

K: That's right. That is the ground upon which everything exists, space . . .

DB: . . . energy . . .

K: . . . energy, emptiness, silence, all that *is*. All that. Not ground, you understand?

DB: No, it is just a metaphor.

K: There is nothing beyond it. No cause. If you have a cause then you have ground.

DB: You have another ground.

K: No. That is the beginning and the ending.

DB: It is becoming more clear.

K: That's right. Does that convey anything to you?

DB: Yes, well I think that it conveys something.

K: Something. Would you say further, there is no beginning and no ending?

DB: Yes. It comes from the ground, goes to the ground, but it does not begin or end.

K: Yes. There is no beginning and no ending. The implications are enormous. Is that death — not death in the sense, I will die, but the complete ending of everything?

DB: You see at first you said that the emptiness is the ending of everything, so in what sense is this more, now? Emptiness is the ending of things, isn't it?

K: Yes, yes. Is that death, this emptiness? Death of everything the mind has cultivated. This emptiness is not the product of the mind, of the particular mind.

DB: No, it is the universal mind.

K: That emptiness is that.

DB: Yes.

K: That emptiness can only exist when there is death — total death — of the particular.

DB: Yes.

K: I don't know if I am conveying this.

DB: Yes, that is the emptiness. But then you are saying that, in this ground, death goes further?

K: Oh, yes.

DB: So we are saying the ending of the particular, the death of the particular, is the emptiness, which is universal. Now are you going to say that the universal also dies?

K: Yes, that is what I am trying to say.

DB: Into the ground.

K: Does it convey anything?

DB: Possibly, yes.

K: Just hold it a minute. Let's see it. I think it conveys something, doesn't it?

DB: Yes. Now if the particular and the universal die, then that is death?

K: Yes. After all, an astronomer says everything in the universe is dying, exploding, dying.

DB: But of course you could suppose that there was something beyond.

K: Yes, that is just it.

DB: I think we are moving. The universal and the particular. First the particular dies into the emptiness, and then comes the universal.

K: And that dies too.

DB: Into the ground, right?

K: Yes.

DB: So you could say the ground is neither born nor dies.

K: That's right.

DB: Well, I think it becomes almost inexpressible if you say the universal is gone, because expression is the universal.

K: You see — I am just explaining: everything is dying, except *that*. Does this convey anything?

DB: Yes. Well it is out of that that everything arises, and into which it dies.

K: So that has no beginning and no ending.

DB: What would it mean to talk of the ending of the universal? What would it mean to have the ending of the universal?

K: Nothing. Why should it have a meaning if it is happening? What has that to do with man? You follow what I mean? Man who is going through a terrible time. What has that got to do with man?

DB: Let's say that man feels he must have some contact with the ultimate ground in his life, otherwise there is no meaning.

K: But it hasn't. That ground hasn't any relationship with man. He is killing himself, he is doing everything contrary to the ground.

DB: Yes, that is why life has no meaning for man.

K: I am an ordinary man; I say, all right, you have talked marvellously of sunsets, but what has that got to do with me? Will that or your talk help me to get over my ugliness? My quarrels with my wife or whatever it is?

DB: I think I would go back, and say we went into this logically starting from the suffering of mankind, showing it originates in a wrong turning, that leads inevitably . . .

K: Yes, but man asks, help me to get past the wrong turn. Put me on the right path. And to that one says, please don't become anything.

DB: Right. What is the problem then?

K: He won't even listen.

DB: Then it seems to me that it is necessary for the one who sees this to find out what is the barrier to listening.

K: Obviously you can see what is the barrier.

DB: What is the barrier?

K: 'I'.

DB: Yes, but I meant more deeply.

K: More deeply, all your thoughts, deep attachments — all that is in your way. If you can't leave these, then you will have no relationship with *that*. But man doesn't want to leave these.

DB: Yes, I understand. What he wants is the result of the way he is thinking.

K: What he wants is some comfortable, easy way of living without any trouble, and he can't have that.

DB: No. Only by dropping all this.

K: There must be a connection. There must be some relationship with the ground and this, some relationship with ordinary man. Otherwise, what is the meaning of living?

DB: That is what I was trying to say before. Without this relationship . . .

K: . . . there is no meaning.

DB: And then people invent meaning.

K: Of course.

DB: Even going back, the ancient religions have said similar things, that God is the ground, so they say seek God, you know.

K: Ah, no, this isn't god.

DB: No, it is not god, but it is saying the same. You could say that 'god' is an attempt to put this notion a bit too personally perhaps.

K: Yes. Give them hope, give them faith, you follow? Make life a little more comfortable to live.

DB: Well, are you asking at this point: how is this to be conveyed to the ordinary man? Is that your question?

K: More or less. And also it is important that he should listen to this. You are a scientist. You are good enough to listen because we are friends. But who will listen among the other scientists? I feel that if one pursues this we will have a marvellously ordered world.

DB: Yes. And what will we do in this world?

K: Live.

DB: But, I mean, we said something about creativity . . .

K: Yes. And then if you have no conflict, no 'I', there is something else operating.

DB: Yes, it is important to say that, because the Christian idea of perfection may seem rather boring because there is nothing to do!

K: We must continue this some other time, because it is something that has got to be put into orbit.

DB: It seems impossible.

K: We have gone pretty far.

2 APRIL 1980, OJAI, CALIFORNIA

THREE

Why Has Man Given Supreme Importance to Thought?

———————————

KRISHNAMURTI: What shall we talk about?

DAVID BOHM: One point relating to what we discussed before; I was reading somewhere that a leading physicist said that the more we understand the universe, the more pointless it seems, the less meaning it has. And it occurred to me that in science there may be an attempt to make the material universe the ground of our existence, so that it may have meaning physically but not . . .

K: . . . any other meaning. Quite.

DB: And the question that we might discuss is this ground which we were talking about the other day. Is it any different to mankind, as the physical universe appears to be?

K: Let's get the question clear.

DB: Not only physicists but geneticists, biologists, have tried to reduce everything to the behaviour of man — atoms, genes, you know, DNA molecules, and so on. And the more they study it, then the more they feel it has no meaning, it is just going on. Though it has meaning physically, in the sense that we can understand it scientifically, it has no deeper meaning than that.

K: I understand that.

DB: And, of course, perhaps that notion has penetrated because in the past people were more religious and felt that the ground of our existence was in something beyond matter — God, or whatever they wished to call it. And that gave them a sense of deep meaning to the whole of their existence, which has now gone away. That is one of the difficulties of modern life, the sense that it doesn't mean anything.

K: So have the religious people *invented* something which has a meaning?

DB: They may well have done so. You see, feeling that life has no meaning, they may have invented something beyond the ordinary. Something which is eternal . . .

K: . . . timeless, nameless.

DB: . . . and independent, absolute.

K: Seeing that the way we live, genetically and all the rest of it, has no meaning, some clever erudite people said, 'We will give it a meaning'.

DB: Well, I think it happened before that. In the past people somehow gave meaning to life, long before science had been very much developed, in the form of religion. And science came along and began to deny this religion.

K: Quite. I understand that.

DB: And people no longer believe in the religious meaning. Perhaps they never were able to believe in it entirely anyway.

K: So, how does one find out if life has a meaning beyond this? How does one find out? They have tried meditation: they have tried every form of self torture, isolation, becoming a monk, a sannyasi and so on. But they may also be deceiving themselves thoroughly.

DB: Yes. And that is in fact why the scientists have denied it all, because the story told by the religious people is no longer plausible, you see.

K: Quite. So how does one find out if there is something more than the mere physical? How would one set about it?

DB: We have been discussing the notion of some ground which is beyond matter, beyond the emptiness.

K: But suppose you say it is so, and I say that is another illusion.

DB: The first point is, perhaps we could clear this up: you see, if this ground is indifferent to human beings, then it would be the same as scientists' ground in matter.

K: Yes. What is the question?

DB: Is the ground indifferent to mankind? You see, the universe appears to be totally indifferent to mankind. It is immense vastness, it pays no attention, it may produce earthquakes and catastrophes, it might wipe things out, it is essentially not interested in mankind.

K: I see what you mean, yes.

DB: It does not care whether man survives or does not survive — if you want to put it that way.

K: Right. I understand the question.

DB: Now I think that people felt that God was a ground who was not indifferent to mankind. You see, they may have invented it, but that is what they believed. And that is what gave them possibly . . .

K: . . . tremendous energy. Quite.

DB: Now I think the point is, would this ground be indifferent to mankind?

K: How would you find out? What is the relationship of this ground to man, and man's relationship to it?

DB: Yes, that is the question. Does man have some significance to it? And does it have significance to man? May I add one more point? I was discussing with somebody who was familiar with the Middle East and traditions of mysticism; he told me that in these traditions they not only say that what we call this ground, this infinite, has some significance, but that what man does has ultimately some significance.

K: Quite, quite. Suppose one says it has — otherwise life has no meaning, nothing has any meaning — how would one find out? Suppose you say this ground exists, as I said the other day. Then the next question is: what relationship has that to man? And man to it? How would one discover, or find out, or touch it — if the ground exists at all? If it doesn't exist, then really man has no meaning at all. I mean, I die and you die and we all die, and what is the point of being virtuous, what is the point of being happy or unhappy, of just carrying on? How would you show that the ground exists? In scientific terms, as well as the feeling of it, the non-verbal communication of it?

DB: When you say scientific do you mean rational?

K: Yes, rational, logical, sane.

DB: So, something that we can actually touch.

K: Not touch, — better than touch — sense. Many can come to it.

DB: Yes, it is public.

K: It isn't just one man's assertion. But it would be scientific. I think it can be shown, but with all things one must *do* it, not just talk about it. Can I — or you — say the ground exists? The ground has certain demands: which are, there must be absolute silence, absolute emptiness, which means no sense of egotism in any form — right? Would you tell me that? Am I willing to let go all my egotism, because I want to prove it, I want to show it, I want to find out if what you are saying is actually true? So am I willing to say, 'Look, complete eradication of the self'?

DB: I think I can say that perhaps in some sense one is willing, but there may be another sense in which the willingness is not subject to one's conscious effort or determination.

K: No, wait. So we go through all that.

DB: We have to see that . . .

K: It is not will, it is not desire, it is not effort.

DB: Yes, but when you say willingness, it contains the word 'will', for example.

K: Willingness, in the sense, go through that door. Or, am I, are we, willing to go through that particular door to find that the ground exists? You ask me that. I say, agreed, I will. I will not in the sense of exercising will and all that. What are the facets or the qualities or the nature of the self? We go into that. You point it out to me and I say, 'Right' — can we do it? Not be attached, not have fear — you follow? — the whole business of it. No belief, absolute rationality — you know — observation. I think if ten people do it, any scientist will accept it. But there are no ten people.

DB: I see. We have to have the thing done together publicly . . .

K: . . . that's it . . .

DB: . . . so that it becomes a real fact.

K: A real fact, in the sense that people accept it. Not something based on illusion, belief, and all the rest of that.

DB: A fact; that which is actually done.

K: Now, who will do this? The scientists want to say that the thing is all illusory, nonsense. But there are others who say, 'It is not nonsense, there *is* a ground. And if you do these things it will be there.'

DB: Yes, but I think that some of the things you say may not in the beginning entirely make sense to the person you talk with.

K: Yes, quite, because he isn't even willing to listen.

DB: But also his whole background is against it. You see, the background gives you the notion of what makes sense and what doesn't. Now, when you say, for example, one of the steps is not to bring in time . . .

K: Ah, that's much more difficult.

DB: Yes, but it is fairly crucial.

K: But wait. I wouldn't begin with time, I would begin at the schoolboy level.

DB: But you are going eventually to reach those more difficult points.

K: Yes. But begin at the schoolboy level and say '*DO* these things.'

DB: Well what are they? Let's go over them.

K: No belief.

DB: A person may not be able to control what he believes, he may not know what he believes.

K: No, don't control anything. Observe that you have belief, you cling to the belief, belief gives you a sense of security and so on. And that belief is an illusion, it has no reality.

DB: You see, I think if we were to talk to scientists like that they might say they were not sure about it, because they believe in the existence of the material world.

K: You don't *believe* the sun rises and sets. It is a fact.

DB: Yes, but the scientist believes. You see, there have been long arguments about this, there is no way to prove that it exists outside my mind, but I believe it anyway. This is one of the questions which arises. Scientists actually have beliefs. One will believe that this theory is right, and the other believes in a different one.

K: No. I have no theories. I don't have any theories. I start at the schoolboy level by saying, 'Look, don't accept theories, conclusions, don't cling to your prejudices.' That is the starting point.

DB: Perhaps we had better say, don't hold to your theories, because somebody might question you if you say you have no theories. They would immediately doubt that, you see.

K: I have no theories. Why should I have theories?

QUESTIONER: If I am a scientist, I would also say I don't have theories. I don't see that the world which I construct for my scientific theories is also theoretical. I would call it fact.

K: So we have to discuss what are facts? Right? I would say that facts are what is happening, actually happening. Would you agree to that?

DB: Yes.

K: Would the scientists agree to that?

DB: Yes. Well, I think that the scientists would say that what is happening is understood through the theories. You see, in science you do not understand what is happening, except with the aid of instruments and theories.

K: Now, wait, wait. What is happening out there, what is happening here?

DB: Let's go slowly. First, what is happening out there. The instruments and theories are needed even to . . .

K: No.

DB: . . . have the facts about what is out there . . .

K: What are the facts out there?

DB: You cannot find out without some kind of theory.

K: The facts there are conflict, why should I have a theory about it?

DB: I wasn't discussing that. I was discussing the facts about matter, you see, which the scientist is concerned with. He cannot establish those facts without a certain theory, because the theory organizes the facts for him.

K: Yes, I understand that. That may be a fact. You may have theories about that.

DB: Yes. About gravitation, atoms — all those things depend on theories in order to produce the right facts.

K: The right facts. So you start with a theory.

DB: A mixture of theory and fact. It is always a combination of theory and fact.

K: All right. A combination of theory and fact.

DB: Now, if you say we are going to have an area where there isn't any such combination . . .

K: That's it. Which is, psychologically I have no theory about myself, about the universe, about my relationship with another. I have no theory. Why should I have? The only fact is, mankind suffers, is miserable, confused, in conflict. That is a fact. Why should I have a theory about it?

DB: You must go slowly. You see, if you are intending to bring in the scientists, this has to be scientific . . .

K: . . . I will go very slowly . . .

DB: . . . so that we don't leave the scientists behind!

K: Quite. Leave me behind!

DB: Well, let's accept 'part company' — right? The scientists might say yes, psychology is the science with which we look inwardly, to investigate the mind. And they say various people — like Freud, and Jung and others — have had theories. Now we will have to make it clear why it has no point to make these theories.

K: Because theory prevents the observation of what is actually taking place.

DB: Yes, but outside it seemed that the theory was helping that observation. Why the difference here?

K: The difference? You can discover that, it is simple.

DB: Let's spell it out. Because if you want to bring in scientists you must answer this question.

K: We will answer it. What is the question?

DB: Why is it that theories are both necessary and useful in organizing facts about matter, outwardly, and yet inwardly, psychologically, they are in the way, they are no use at all.

K: Yes. What is theory? The meaning of the word, theory?

DB: Theory means to see, to view, a kind of insight.

K: To view? That's it. A way of looking.

DB: And the theory helps you to look at the outside matter.

K: Theory means to observe.

DB: It is a way of observing.

K: Can you observe psychologically what is going on?

DB: Let's say that when we look at matter outwardly, to a certain extent we fix the observing.

K: That is, the observer is different from the observed.

DB: Not only different, but their relationship is fixed, relatively at least, for some time.

K: So we can move now, a little.

DB: This appears to be necessary in order to study matter. Matter does not change so fast, and it can be separated to some extent. We can then make a fairly constant way of looking. It changes but not immediately, it can be held constant for a while.

K: Yes.

DB: And we call that theory.

K: As you said, theory means a way of observing.

DB: It is the same as 'theatre' in Greek.

K: Theatre, yes, that's right. It is a way of looking. Now, where do we start? A common way of looking, an ordinary way of looking, the way of looking depending on the viewpoint of each person — the housewife, the husband? What do you mean by the way of looking?

DB: The same problem arose in the development of science. We began with what was called commonsense, a common way of looking. Then scientists discovered that this was inadequate.

K: They moved away from it.

DB: They moved away, they gave up some parts of it.

K: That is what I am coming to. The common way of looking is full of prejudice.

DB: Yes, it is arbitrary, and dependent on your background.

K: Yes, all that. So can one be free of one's background, one's prejudice? I think one can.

DB: The question is whether a theory of psychology would be any help in doing this. The danger is that the theory itself might be a prejudice. If you tried to make a theory . . .

K: That is what I am saying. That would become a prejudice.

DB: That would become a prejudice because we have nothing — we have not yet observed anything to found it on.

K: So the common factor is that man suffers — right? That is the common factor. And the way of observing matters.

DB: Yes. I wonder whether scientists would accept that as the most fundamental factor of man.

K: All right. Conflict?

DB: Well, they have argued about it.

K: Take anything, it doesn't matter. Attachment, pleasure, fear.

DB: I think some people might object, saying we should take something more positive.

K: Which is what?

DB:　Simply, for example, some people might have said that rationality is a common factor.

K:　No, no, no! I won't call rationality a common factor. If people were rational they wouldn't be fighting each other.

DB:　We have to make this clear. Let's say in the past somebody like Aristotle might have said rationality is the common factor of man. Now your argument against it is that men are not generally rational.

K:　No, they are not.

DB:　Though they might be, they are not. So you are saying that is not a fact.

K:　That's right.

Q:　I think commonly scientists would say that there are many different human beings and that the common factor of mankind is that they are all striving for happiness.

K:　Is that the common factor? No. I won't accept that — that many human beings are trying for happiness.

Q:　No. Human beings are all different.

K:　Agreed. Stay there.

Q:　What I am saying is that this is the common theory, which people believe to be a fact.

K:　That is, each person thinks he is totally different from others.

Q:　Yes. And they are all independently struggling for happiness.

K:　They are all seeking some kind of gratification. Would you agree to that?

DB:　That is one common factor. But the reason I brought up rationality was that the very existence of science is based on the notion that rationality is common to man.

K:　But each person is seeking his own individuality.

DB:　But, you see, science would be impossible if that were entirely true.

K:　Quite.

Q: Why?

DB: Because everybody would not be interested in the truth. The very possibility of scientific discovery depends on people feeling that this common goal of finding the truth is beyond personal satisfaction, because even if your theory is wrong you must accept that it is wrong, though it is not gratifying. That is, it becomes very disappointing for people, but they accept it, and say, well, that is wrong.

K: I am not seeking gratification. I am a common man. You have brought up that scientists take for granted that human beings are rational.

DB: At least when they do science. They may agree that they are not very rational in private life, but they say that at least they are capable of being rational when they do scientific work. Otherwise it would be impossible to begin.

K: So outwardly, in dealing with matter, they are all rational.

DB: At least they try to be, and they are to some extent.

K: They try to be, but they become irrational in their relationships with other human beings.

DB: Yes. They cannot maintain it.

K: So that is the common factor.

DB: Yes. It is important to bring out this point — that rationality is limited, and, as you say, the fundamental fact is that more generally they cannot be rational. They may succeed in some limited area.

K: That's right. That is a fact.

DB: That is a fact, though we don't say it is inevitable, or that it can't be changed.

K: No. It is a fact.

DB: It is a fact that it has been, it has happened, it is happening.

K: Yes. I, as a common human being, have been irrational. And my life has been totally contradictory, and so on, which is irrational. Now can I as a human being change that?

DB: Let's see how we could proceed from the scientific approach. This would raise the question, why is everybody irrational?

K: Because we have been conditioned that way. Our education, our religion, our everything.

DB: But that won't get us anywhere, because it leads to more questions: how did we get conditioned and so on

K: We can go into all that.

DB: But I meant that following that line is not going to answer.

K: Quite. Why are we conditioned that way?

DB: For example, we were saying the other day that perhaps man took a wrong turning, established the wrong conditioning.

K: The wrong conditioning from the beginning. Or, seeking security — security for myself, for my family, for my group, for my tribe — has brought about this division.

DB: Even then you have to ask why man sought this security in the wrong way. You see, if there had been any intelligence, it would have been clear that this whole thing has no meaning.

K: Of course, you are going back to taking the wrong turn. How will you show me we have taken a wrong turning?

DB: Are you saying that we want to demonstrate this scientifically?

K: Yes. I think the wrong turn was taken when thought became all important.

DB: What made it all important?

K: Now let's work it out. What made human beings enthrone thought as the only means of operation?

DB: Also it would have to be made clear why, if thought is so important, it causes all the difficulties. These are the two questions.

K: That is fairly simple. So thought has been made king, supreme. And that may be the wrong turn of human beings.

DB: You see, I think that thought became the equivalent of truth. People took thought to give truth, to give what is always true. There is the notion that we have knowledge — which may hold in certain cases for some time — but men generalize, because knowledge is always generalizing. When they got to the notion that it would always be so, this crystallized the thought of what is true. This gave thought supreme importance.

K: You are asking, aren't you, why has man given thought such importance?

DB: I think he has slipped into it.

K: Why?

DB: Because he did not see what he was doing. You see, in the beginning he did not see the danger . . .

Q: Just before, you said that the common ground for man is reason . . .

K: Scientists say that.

Q: If you can show a person that something is true . . .

K: Show it to me. It is true I am irrational. That is a fact, that is truth.

Q: But for that you don't need reason. Observation is sufficient for that.

K: No. One goes and fights. One talks about peace. One is irrational. Dr. Bohm is pointing out that scientists say man is rational but the fact is that everyday life is irrational. Now we are asking, show us scientifically why it is irrational. That is, show man in what way he has slipped into this irrationality; why human beings have accepted this. We can say it is habit, tradition, religion. And the scientists also, they are very rational in their own field, but irrational in their lives.

Q: And you suggested that making thought the king is the main irrationality?

K: That is right. We have reached that point.

DB: But how did we slip into making thought so important?

K: Why has man given importance to thought as the supreme thing? I think that is fairly easy. Because that is the only thing he knows.

DB: It doesn't follow that he would give it supreme importance.

K: Because the things I know — the things thought has created, the images, all the rest of it — are more important than the things I don't know.

DB: But you see, if intelligence were operating he would not come to that conclusion. It is not rational to say that all that I know is all that is important.

K: So, man is irrational.

DB: He slipped into irrationality to say, all that I know is all that is important. But why should man have done this?

K: Would you say that the mistake is made because he clings to the known, and objects to anything unknown?

DB: That is a fact, but it is not clear why he should.

K: Because that is the only thing he has.

DB: But I am asking why he was not intelligent enough to see this.

K: Because he is irrational.

DB: Well, we are going around in circles!

K: I don't think so.

DB: Look, every one of these reasons you give is merely another example of man's irrationality.

K: That is all I am saying. We are basically irrational, because we have given thought supreme importance.

Q: But the step before that is that the thought has built up the idea that I exist?

K: Ah, that comes a little later; we have to go step by step.

Q: Surely for the 'me', the only thing that exists is thought.

K: Would the scientists accept that?

DB: The scientist feels he is investigating the real nature of matter, independent of thought, ultimately independent anyway. He wants to know the way the universe is. He may be fooling himself, but he feels that it wouldn't be worth doing unless he believes he is finding an objective fact.

K: So would you say that through the investigation of matter he is trying to find something, he is trying to find the ground?

DB: That's exactly it.

K: But wait! *Is* that it?

DB: Precisely, yes.

K: Now the religious man says you cannot find it by becoming terribly rational in your life. He doesn't accept that he is rational but says he is irrational in contradiction, and so on. So either he will have to clear up that first — step by step, or he can do the whole thing at one blow. Right? One accepts that one is irrational.

DB: But there is a difficulty. If you accept you are irrational, you stop, because you say, how can you begin?

K: Yes. But if I accept I *am* irrational — wait a minute — completely, then I am rational!

DB: You will have to make that more clear. You could say that man has been deluding himself into believing that he is already rational.

K: I don't accept that.

DB: Now if you don't accept this delusion, then you are saying that rationality will be there.

K: No, I don't accept it. The *fact* is, I am irrational and, to find the ground, I must become extremely rational in my life. That's all. Irrationality has been brought about by thought creating this idea of me as separate from everybody else. So can I, being irrational, find the cause of irrationality and wipe it out? If I can't do that, I cannot reach the ground which is *the* most rational. Would a scientist who is investigating matter accept that the ground exists at all?

DB: Well, tacitly he is assuming that it does.

K: It does. Mr. 'X' comes along and says it *does* exist. And you, the scientists, say, 'Show it.' Mr. 'X' says, I will show it to you. A scientist meets with other scientists, experimenting and being rational in that area, although irrational in his own life. First become rational in your life, begin here, rather than there. What would you say to all that? This must be done without effort, without desire, without will, without any sense of persuasion; otherwise you are back in the game.

DB: Let's try to put it like this: even in science you could not pursue the science fully unless you were rational.

K: Somewhat rational.

DB: Somewhat rational, but, eventually, the failure of rationality blocks science anyway. Scientists cling to their theories, and they become jealous and so on.

K: That's it, that is all. The irrationality overcomes them.

DB: So then you could say you might as well look at the source of the whole irrationality.

K: That is what I am saying.

DB: But now you have to make it clear that it really can be done.

K: Oh yes, I am showing it to you. I say, first recognize, see, observe, be aware that you are totally irrational.

DB: The word 'totally' will cause trouble, because if you were totally irrational you couldn't even begin to talk.

K: No, that is my question. I say one is totally irrational. First, recognize it. Watch it. The moment you admit there is some part of me that is rational, who wants to wipe away the irrationality . . .

DB: . . . It is not that, but there must be sufficient rationality to understand what you are talking about.

K: Yes, of course.

DB: Essentially, I would rather put it that one is dominated by one's irrationality, even though there is enough rationality to discuss the question.

K: I question that.

DB: You see, otherwise we couldn't begin to talk.

K: But listen. We begin to talk. A few of us begin to talk because we are willing to listen to each other, we are willing to say, we'll set aside any conclusions we have; we are willing to listen to each other.

DB: That is part of rationality.

K: With some of us perhaps, but the vast majority is not willing to listen to us, because we are concerned, serious enough to find out if the ground exists. That gives us rationality to listen to each other.

DB: Listening is necessary for rationality.

K: Of course. Are we saying the same thing?

DB: Yes.

K: The scientist, through the examination of matter, hopes to reach the ground. We and 'X' and 'Y' say, let us become rational in our life. Which means that you and I, and 'X' and 'Y' are willing to listen to each other. That's all. The very listening is the beginning of rationality. Some people won't listen to us or to anybody. So can we, who *are* listening, be somewhat rational, and begin? That is all my point. This is being terribly logical, isn't it? So can we proceed from there?

Why has man brought about this irrationality in his life? A few of us can apparently throw off some part of irrationality, become somewhat rational and say, now, let's start. Let us start to find out why man lives this way. Now what is the common dominant factor in all our lives? Obviously it is thought.

DB: Yes, that is so. Of course many people might deny that and say it is feeling, or that something else is the major factor.

K: Many people might say that, but thought is part of feeling.

DB: Yes, but that is not commonly understood.

K: We will explain it. Feeling — if there was no thought behind it, would you be able to recognize it?

DB: Yes, I think this is a major difficulty, in communication with some people.

K: So we begin. There may be some who don't see this, but I want the free 'X' and 'Y' to see it, because they have become somewhat rational, therefore they are listening to each other. They can say thought is the main source of this current.

DB: Then we have to say, what is thought?

K: I think that is fairly simple. Thought brings about irrationality.

DB: Yes, but what is it? How do you know you are thinking? What do you mean by thinking?

K: Thinking is the movement of memory, which is experience, knowledge, stored in the brain.

DB: Suppose we want to have rationality which includes rational thought. Is rational thought only memory?

K: Wait a minute. Let's be careful. If we are completely rational, there is total insight. That insight uses thought, and then it is rational.

DB: Then thought is not only memory?

K: No, no.

DB: Well, I mean since it is being used by insight . . .

K: No, insight uses thought.

DB: Yes, but what thought does is not just due to memory now.

K: Wait a minute.

DB: Outwardly thought runs on its own, it runs like a machine on its own, and it is not rational.

K: Quite right.

DB: But when thought is the instrument of insight . . .

K: Then thought is not memory.

DB: It is not based on memory.

K: No, not based on memory.

DB: Memory is used, but it is not based on memory.

K: Then what? Thought being limited, divisive, incomplete, can never be rational . . .

DB: Without insight.

K: That's right. Now, how are we to have insight which is total rationality? Not the rationality of thought.

DB: I should call it rationality of perception.

K: Yes, rationality of perception.

DB: Then thought becomes the instrument of that, so it has the same order.

K: Now how am I to have that insight? That is the next question. Isn't it? What am I to do, or not to do, to have this instant insight, which is not of time, which is not of memory, which has no cause, which is not based on reward or punishment? It is free of all that. Now how does the mind have this insight? When I say, I have the insight, that is wrong. Obviously. So how is it possible for a mind which has been irrational, and has become somewhat rational, to have that insight? It is possible to have that insight if your mind is free from time.

DB: Right. Let's go slowly because you see, if we go back to the scientific, even commonsense point of view, implicitly time is taken as the ground of everything in scientific work. In fact even in ancient Greek mythology Chronos, the god of time, produces his children and swallows them. That is exactly what we said about the ground; everything comes from the ground and dies to the ground. So, in a way, mankind long ago began to take time already as the ground.

K: Yes. And then someone comes along and says time is not the ground.

DB: That's right. So until now even scientists have been looking for the ground in time — and everybody else too!

K: That is the whole point.

DB: Now you say time is not the ground. Somebody might say this is nonsense, but we say, we will stay open to that, although some people might easily dismiss it right away. Now if you say time is not the ground, we don't know where we are.

K: I know where I am. We will go into it.

Q: Is time the same movement as this thought which we described first?

K: Yes, time is that. Time is thought.

DB: Let's go slowly again on that, because there is, as we have often said, chronological time.

K: Of course, that is simple.

DB: Yes, but in addition we are thinking. You see, thinking takes time chronologically, but in addition it projects a kind of imaginary time . . .

K: . . . which is the future.

DB: Which is the future and the past as we experience it.

K: Yes, that is right.

DB: That time which is imagined is also a kind of real process of thinking.

K: It is a fact.

DB: It is a fact that it takes time, physically, to think, but we also have time when we can imagine the whole past and future.

K: Yes, which are facts.

DB: So let's say that this time is not the ground, perhaps not even physically.

K: We are going to find out.

DB: Yes, but we feel it to be the ground, because we feel that we, as the self, exist in time. Without time there could be no 'me'.

K: That's it.

DB: 'I' must exist in time.

K: Of course, of course.

DB: Eternally being something, or becoming something.

K: Becoming and being are in the field of time. Now can the mind, which has evolved through time . . .

Q: What do you mean by mind then?

K: Mind — the brain, my senses, my feeling, all that is the mind.

DB: The particular mind, you mean.

K: Particular mind, of course, I am talking of the mind that has evolved through time.

DB: Even its particularity depends on time.

K: Time, of course, and all the rest of it. Now we are asking, can that mind be free of time, to have an insight which is totally rational, which then can operate on thought? That thought is totally rational, not based on memory. Agreed?

DB: Yes.

K: Now how am I — as 'X' and 'Y' — to be free of time? I know I need time to go from here to there, to learn a lesson, a technique, etc. I understand that very clearly, so I am not talking about that time. I am talking about time as becoming.

DB: As being.

K: Of course, becoming is being. I start from being to become.

DB: And being something in myself. Being better, being happier.

K: Yes, the whole thing — the more. Now can I, can my brain investigating to find out if the ground exists, can my whole mind be free of time? We have now separated time. The time which is necessary, and the time which is not necessary. That is, can my brain not function as it has always done, in time as thought? Which means, can thought come to an end? Would you accept that?

DB: Yes, but could you make that more clear? We can see that the first question is, can my brain not be dominated by the function of thought?

K: Yes, which is time.

DB: And then, if you say thought comes to an end . . .

K: No! Can time as thought come to a stop?

DB: Psychological time comes to a stop.

K: Yes, I am talking of that.

DB: But we will still have the rational thought.

K: Of course. That is understood. We have said that.

DB: We are discussing the thought of conscious experience.

Q: Of becoming and being . . .

K: And the retention of memory; you know, the past, as knowledge. Oh, yes, that can be done.

DB: You really mean the memory of experiences?

K: The memory of experiences, hurts, attachments, the whole of it. Now can that come to an end? Of course it can. This is the point: it can come to an end when the very perception asks, what is it? What is hurt? What is psychological damage? The perception of it *is* the ending of it. Not carrying it over, which is time. The very ending of it is the ending of time. I think that is clear. 'X' is hurt, wounded from childhood. And he, by listening, talking, discussing, realizes that the continuation of the hurt is time. And to find out the ground, time must end. So he says, can my hurt end instantly, immediately?

DB: Yes, I think there are some steps in that. You say, he finds that hurt is time, but the immediate experience of it is that it exists on its own.

K: I know, of course. We can go into that.

DB: That simply is something on its own.

K: Which means, I have created an image about myself and the image is hurt, but not me.

DB: What do you mean by that?

K: All right. In the becoming, which is time, I have created an image about myself.

DB: Well, thought has created that image.

K: Thought has created an image through experience, through education, through conditioning, and made this image separate -from me. But this image is actually 'me', although we have separated the image and the me, which is irrational. So, in realizing that the image *is* 'me', I have become somewhat rational.

DB: I think that will not be clear — because if I am hurt I feel the image is 'me'.

K: The image *is* you.

DB: The person who is hurt feels that way, you see.

K: All right. But the moment you operate on it you separate yourself.

DB: That's the point. Now the first feeling is that the image is 'me' hurt, and the second feeling is that I draw back from the image in order to operate on it . . .

K: . . . which is irrationality.

DB: . . . because it is not correct.

K: That's right.

DB: And that brings in time, because I say it will take time to do that.

K: Quite right. So by seeing that, I become rational, and act. The act is to be free of it immediately.

DB: Let's go into that. The first thing is that there has been a hurt. That is the image, but at first I don't separate it. I feel identified with it.

K: I am that.

DB: I am that. But then I draw back, and say that I think there must be a 'me' who can do something.

K: Yes, can operate on it.

DB: Now that takes time.

K: That is time.

DB: That is time, but I mean, I am thinking it takes time. Now I have to go slowly. If I don't do that, that hurt cannot exist.

K: That's right.

DB: But it is not obvious in the experience itself that this is so.

K: First let's go slowly into it. I am hurt. That is a fact. Then I separate myself — there is a separation — saying, I will do something about it.

DB: The 'me' who will do something is different.

K: Different, of course.

DB: And he thinks about what he should do.

K: The 'me' is different because it is becoming.

DB: It projects into the future a different state.

K: Yes. I am hurt. There is a separation, a division. The 'me', which is always pursuing the becoming, says, I must control it. I must wipe it out. I must act upon it, or I will be vengeful, hurtful. So this movement of separation is time.

DB: We can see that now. The point is, there is something here that is not obvious. A person is thinking that the hurt exists independently of 'me', and I must do something about it. I project into the future the better state and what I will do. Let's try to make this very clear, because you are saying that there is no separation.

K: My rationality discovers there is no separation.

DB: There is no separation, but the illusion that there is a separation helps to maintain the hurt.

K: That's right. Because the illusion is, I am becoming.

DB: Yes. I am this and will become that. So I am hurt and I will become non-hurt. Now that very thought maintains the hurt.

K: That's right.

Q: Is the separation not already there when I become conscious and say I am hurt?

K: I am hurt. Then I say, I am going to hit you because you have hurt me, or I say, I must suppress it — or I create fear, and so on.

Q: But isn't that feeling of separation there from the moment I say I am hurt?

K: That is irrationality.

Q: That is irrational already?

K: Yes, when you say, does not the separation exist already when I say 'I am hurt'.

DB: It does, but I think that before that happens you get a kind of shock. The first thing that happens is a mild shock, a pain or whatever, which you identify with that shock. Then you explain it by saying 'I am hurt', and that immediately implies the separation to do something about it.

K: Of course. If I am not hurt I don't know anything about separation or not separation. If I am hurt, I am irrational as long as I maintain that hurt and do something about it, which is to become. Then irrationality comes in. I think that is right.

DB: Now if you don't maintain it, what happens? Suppose you say, I won't go on with this becoming?

K: Ah, that is quite a different matter. It means I am no longer thinking, no longer observing, or using time as an observation.

DB: You could say that is not your way of looking. It is not your theory any more.

K: That's right.

DB: Because you could say time is a theory which everybody adopts for psychological purposes.

K: Yes. That is the common factor; time is the common factor of man. And we are pointing out time is an illusion . . .

DB: Psychological time.

K: Of course, that is understood.

DB: Are you saying that when we no longer approach this through time, then the hurt does not continue?

K: It does not continue, it ends — because you are not becoming anything.

DB: In becoming you are always continuing what you are.

K: That's right. Continuing what you are, modified . . .

DB: That is why you struggle to become.

K: We are talking about insight. That is, insight has no time. Insight is not the product of time, time being memory, etc. So there is insight. That insight being free of time acts upon memory, acts upon thought. That is, insight makes thought rational, but not thought which is based on memory. Then what the devil is that thought?

No. Wait a minute. I don't think thought comes in at all. We said insight comes into being when there is no time. Thought — which is based on memory, experience, knowledge — that is the movement of time as becoming. We are talking of psychological and not chronological time. We are saying to be free of time implies insight. Insight, being free of time, has no thought.

DB: We said that it may use thought.

K: Wait. I am not sure. Just go slowly. It may use thought to explain, but it acts. Before, action was based on thought. Now, when there is insight, there is only action. Why do you want thought? Because insight is rational, action is rational. Action becomes irrational when it is acting from thought. So insight doesn't use thought.

DB: Well, we have to make it clear because in a certain area it has to use thought. . . . If, for example, you want to construct something you would use the thought which is available on how to do it.

K: But that is not insight.

DB: But even so you may have to have insight in that area.

K: Partial. The scientists, the painters, the architects, the doctors, the artists and so on have partial insight. But we are talking of 'X' and 'Y', who are seeking the ground; they are becoming rational, and we are saying insight is without time, and therefore without thoughts, and that insight is action. Because that insight is rational, action is rational. Forgive me, I am not making myself an example, I am talking in all humility. That boy, that young man in 1929 dissolved the Order of the Star. There was no thought. People said, 'Do this', 'Don't do that', 'Keep it', 'Don't keep it'. He had an insight; dissolved it. Finished! Why do we need thought?

DB: But then you used some thought in dissolving the Order to say, when to do it, how to do it.

K: That word is used merely for convenience, for communication with other people.

DB: But still some thought was needed.

K: The decision acts.

DB: I didn't mean about the decision. The primary action did not require thought; only that which followed.

K: That is nothing. It is like moving a cushion from there to there.

DB: Yes, I understand that. Then the primary source of action does not involve thought.

K: That is all I wanted to say.

DB: But it sort of filters through into . . .

K: . . . it is like a wave.

Q: Does not all thought undergo a transformation in this process?

K: Yes, of course. Because insight is without time, therefore the brain itself has undergone a change.

DB: Yes, now could we talk about what you mean by that?

K: Does it mean that every human response must be viewed by, or must enter into insight? I will tell you what I mean. I am jealous. Is there an insight which will cover the whole field of jealousy and so end it? End envy, greed, and all that is involved in jealousy. You follow? Irrational people go step by step — get rid of jealousy, get rid of attachment, get rid of anger, get rid of this, that and the other. Which is a constant process of becoming — right? But insight, which is totally rational, wipes all that away.

DB: Right.

K: Is that a fact? Fact, in the sense that 'X' and 'Y' will never be jealous again; *never!*

DB: We have to discuss that, because it is not clear how you could guarantee it.

K: Oh, yes, I will guarantee it!

DB: If it can reach those who are able to listen. . . .

K: Which means that to find the ground the first thing is to listen.

DB: You see, scientists cannot always listen. Even Einstein and Bohr were not able at a certain point to listen to each other. Each one was attached to his particular view.

K: They brought their irrationality into operation.

8 APRIL 1980, OJAI, CALIFORNIA

FOUR

Breaking the Pattern of Ego-centred Activity

KRISHNAMURTI: I would like to ask a question which may lead us to something: what will make man change, deeply, fundamentally, radically? He has had crisis after crisis, he has had a great many shocks, he has been through every kind of misfortune, every kind of war, personal sorrow, and so on. A little affection, a little joy, but all this doesn't seem to change him. What will make a human being leave the way he is going, and move in a totally different direction? I think that is one of our great problems, don't you? Why? If one is concerned, as one must be, with humanity, with all the things that are going on, what would be the right action to move man out of one direction to another? Is this question valid? Has it any significance?

DAVID BOHM: Well, unless we can see this action, it won't have much significance.

K: Has the question any significance?

DB: What it means is, indirectly, to ask what is holding people.

K: Yes, same thing.

DB: If we could find out what is holding people in their present direction . . .

K: Is it the basic conditioning of man, this tremendous egotistic attitude and action, which won't yield to anything? It appears to change, it appears to yield, but the centre remains the same. Perhaps this may not be in the line of our dialogue over the last two or three days, but I thought we might start with this.

DB: Have you some notion of what is holding people? Something that would really change them?

K: I think so.

DB: What is it then?

K: What is it that is blocking? Do we approach through environmental conditioning, from the outer to the inner, and discover from man's outer activities, the inner? And then discover that the outer is the inner, the same movement, and then go beyond it to see what it is? Could we do that?

DB: When you say outward, what do you mean? Do you mean the social conditions?

K: The social conditioning, the religious conditioning, education, poverty, riches, climate, food; the outer. Which may condition the mind in a certain direction. But as one examines it a little more, the psychological conditioning is also from the outer, somewhat.

DB: It is true that the way a person thinks is going to be affected by his whole set of relationships. But that doesn't explain why the conditioning is so rigid, and why it holds.

K: That is what I am asking too.

DB: Yes. If it were merely outward conditioning, one would expect it to be more easily changed. For example, you could have some other outward condition.

K: They have tried all that.

DB: Yes, the whole belief of Communism was that with a new society there would be a new man. But there have been none! I think that there is something fundamentally in the inward that holds, that resists change.

K: What is it? Will this question lead us anywhere?

DB: Unless we actually uncover it, it will lead nowhere.

K: I think one could find out, if one applied one's mind. I am just asking: is this question worth-while, and is it related to what we have been discussing? Or shall we take up something else in relation to what we have been talking about?

DB: Well, I think that we have been talking of bringing about an ending to time, an ending to becoming. And we talked of coming into contact with the ground, through complete rationality. But now we could say that the mind is not rational.

K: Yes, we said man is basically irrational.

DB: This is perhaps part of the block. If we were completely rational, then we would of necessity come to this ground. Would that be right?

K: Yes. We were talking the other day about the ending of time. The scientists, through the investigation of matter, want to find out that point. Also the so-called religious people have endeavoured to find out — not only verbally — if time can stop. We went into that quite a bit, and we say it *is* possible for a human being, who will listen, to find out through insight the ending of time. Because insight is not memory. Memory is time, memory is experience, knowledge stored up in the brain, and so on. As long as that is in operation there is no possibility of having insight into anything. Total insight, not partial insight. The artist, the scientist, the musician, they all have partial insights and therefore they are still time-bound.

Is it possible to have a total insight, which is the ending of the 'me', because the 'me' is time? Me, my ego, my resistance, my hurts, all that. Can that 'me' end? It is only when that ends that there is total insight. That is what we discovered.

And we went into the question, is it possible for a human being to end totally this whole structure of the 'me'? We said yes, and went into it. Very few people will listen to this because it is perhaps too frightening. And the question then arises: if the 'me' ends, what is there? Just emptiness? There is no interest in that. But if one is investigating without any sense of reward or punishment, then there is something. We say that something is total emptiness, which is energy and silence. Well that sounds nice, but it has no meaning to an ordinary man who is serious and wants to go beyond it, beyond himself. And we pushed it further: is there something beyond all this? And we say there is.

DB: The ground.

K: The ground. Is it that the beginning of this enquiry is to listen? Will I, as a human being, give up my egocentric activity completely? What will make me move away from that? What will make a human being move away from this destructive, self-centred activity? If he will move away through reward, or punishment, then that is just another thought, motive. So discard that. Then what will make human beings renounce — if I may use the word — renounce it completely without motive?

You see, man has tried everything in this direction — fasting, self-torture in various forms, abnegating himself through belief and denying himself through identification with something greater. All the religious people have tried it, but the 'me' is still there.

DB: Yes. The whole activity has no meaning, but somehow this does not become evident. People will move away from something which has no meaning, and makes no sense, ordinarily speaking. But it seems that the perception of this fact is rejected by the mind. The mind is resisting it.

K: The mind is resisting this constant conflict, and moving away from it.

DB: It is moving away from the fact that this conflict has no meaning.

K: People don't see that.

DB: Also the mind is set up purposefully to avoid seeing it.

K: The mind is avoiding it.

DB: It is avoiding it almost on purpose, but not quite consciously, like the people of India who say they are going to retire to the Himalayas because nothing can be done.

K: But that is hopeless. You mean to say that the mind, having lived so long in conflict, refuses to move away from it?

DB: It is not clear why it refuses to give it up; why the mind does not wish to see the full meaninglessness of the conflict. The mind is deceiving itself, it is covering up.

K: The philosophers and so-called religious people have emphasized struggle, emphasized the sense of striving, control, effort. Is that one of the causes why human beings refuse to let go of their way of life?

DB: Possibly. They hope that by fighting or struggling they will achieve a better result. Not to give up what they have, but to improve it by struggle.

K: Man has lived for two million years; what has he achieved? More wars, more destruction.

DB: What I am trying to say is that there is a tendency to resist seeing this, but also to go back to hoping that the struggle will produce something better.

K: I am not quite sure if we have cleared this point; that the intellectuals — I am using the word respectfully — the intellectuals of the world have emphasized this factor of struggle.

DB: Many of them have, I suppose.

K: Most of them.

DB: Karl Marx.

K: Marx and even Bronowski, who talk of more and more struggle, of acquiring more and more knowledge. Is it that the intellectuals have such extraordinary influence on our minds?

DB: I think people do this without any encouragement from intellectuals. You see, struggle has been emphasized everywhere.

K: That is what I mean. Everywhere. Why?

DB: Well, in the beginning people thought it would be necessary because they had to struggle against nature in order to survive.

K: So struggling against nature has been transferred to the other?

DB: Yes, that is part of it. You see you must be a brave hunter, and you must struggle against your own weakness to become brave. Otherwise you can't do it.

K: Yes, that's it. So is it that our minds are conditioned, shaped, held, in this pattern?

DB: Well that is certainly true, but it doesn't explain why it is so extraordinarily hard to change it.

K: Because I am used to it. I am in a prison, but I am used to it.

DB: But I think that there is a tremendous resistance to moving away from it.

K: Why does a human being resist this? If you come along and point out the fallacy, the irrationality of this, and you show the whole cause and effect, give examples, data, everything else? Why?

DB: That is what I said, that if people were capable of complete rationality they would drop it, but I think that there is something more to the problem. You see, you may expose the irrationality of it but there is something more, in the sense that people are not fully aware of this whole pattern of thought. Having had it exposed at a certain level, it still continues at levels that they are not aware of.

K: But what would make them aware?

DB: That is what we have to find. I think people have to become aware that they have this tendency to go on with the conditioning. It might be mere habit, or it might be the result of many past conclusions, all operating *now*, without people knowing it. There are so many different things that keep people in this pattern. You might convince somebody that the pattern makes no sense, but when it comes to the actual affairs of life he has a thousand different ways of proceeding which imply that pattern.

K: Quite. Then what?

DB: Well, I think that a person would have to be extremely interested in this to break all that down.

K: Then what will bring a human being to this state of extreme interest? You see, they have even been offered heaven as a reward if they do this. Various religions have done this, although that becomes too childish.

DB: That is part of the pattern — reward. Ordinarily the rule is that I follow the self-enclosed pattern except when something really big comes up.

K: A crisis.

DB: Or when a reward is to be obtained.

K: Of course.

DB: That is a pattern of thinking. People must in some way believe that it has value. If everybody were able to work together and suddenly we were able to produce harmony, then everybody would say, fine, I will give up myself. But in the absence of that, I had better hold on to what I have! That is the sort of thinking.

K: Hold on to what is known.

DB: I don't have much, but I had better hold on to it.

K: Yes. So are you saying that if everybody does this, I will do it?

DB: That is the common way of thinking. Because as soon as people begin to start to cooperate in an emergency, then a great many people go along.

K: So they form communes. But all those have failed.

DB: Because after a while this special thing goes away and they fall back to the old pattern.

K: The old pattern. So I am asking, what will make a human being break through this pattern?

QUESTIONER: Isn't it related to the question we dealt with before — time and no time?

K: But I know nothing about time, I know nothing about all this, it is just a theory to me. Yet the fact is, I am caught in this pattern and I can't let it go. The analysts have tried it, the religious people have tried it, everybody has tried to make human beings intelligent — but they have not succeeded.

Q: But they don't see that the very attempt at letting go the pattern or ending the conflict is still strengthening the conflict.

K: No, that is just a theory.

Q: But you can explain that to them.

K: You can explain. As we said, there are a dozen very rational explanations. At the end of it we fall back to this.

Q: Well, you only fall back to that if you have not really understood it.

K: Have *you* understood it when you say that? Why haven't I, or you, said 'finished'! You can give me a thousand explanations, and all probably a bit irrational, but I say, have you done it?

Q: I don't even understand the question, when you ask, have I done it?

K: I am not being personal. You have given an explanation of why human beings can't move away from this pattern, or break through it.

Q: No, I give you more than the explanation.

K: What do you give me?

Q: If I observe something to be correct, then the description of the observation is more than just explanation.

K: Yes, but can I observe this clearly?

Q: Well, that is the problem.

K: So help me to see it clearly.

Q: For that there must be an interest.

K: Please don't say 'must'. I haven't got an interest. I am interested, as Dr. Bohm pointed out just now, when there is a tremendous crisis such as war. Then I forget myself. In fact, I am glad to forget myself, to give the responsibility to the generals, to the politicians. Under a crisis I forget, but the moment the crisis goes away I am back to my pattern. That is happening all the time. Now, I say to myself, what will make me relinquish this pattern, or break through it?

Q: Isn't it that one must see the falseness?

K: *Show* it to me.

Q: I can't, because I have not seen it.

K: Then what shall I do as a human being? You have explained to me ten thousand times how ugly it is, how destructive it is, and so on, but I fall back to this pattern all the time. Help me, or show me how to break the pattern. You understand my question?

Q: Well then you are interested?

K: All right. Now what will make me be interested? Pain?

Q: Sometimes it does for a moment, but it goes away.

K: So what will make me as a human being so alert, so aware, so intense that I will break through this thing?

Q: You state the question in terms of an action, breaking through, relinquishing. Isn't it a matter of seeing?

K: Yes. Show me, help me to see, because I am resisting you. My pattern, so deeply ingrained in me, is holding back — right? I want proof, I want to be convinced.

Q: We have to go back to this question — why do I want to have proof? Why do I want to be convinced?

K: Because someone says that this is a stupid, irrational way of looking. And he shows us all the effects of it, the cause of it, and we say, yes but we can't let go!

DB: You may say that is the very nature of 'me', that I must fulfil my needs no matter how irrational they are.

K: That is what I am saying.

DB: First I must take care of my own needs, and then I can try to be rational.

K: What are our needs then?

DB: Some of the needs are real and some are imaginary but . . .

K: Yes, that's it. The imaginary, illusory needs sway the other needs.

DB: But you see, I may need to believe I am good and right, and to know that I will be always there.

K: Help me to break that!

DB: I think I have to see that this is an illusion. You see, if it seems real, what can I do? Because if I am really there, I need all this, and it is foolish to talk of being rational if I am going to vanish, break down or something. You have proposed to me that there is another state of being where I am not there — right? And when I *am* there, this doesn't make any sense!

K: Yes, quite. But I am *not* there. Suppose as a human being, heaven is perfect, but I am not there; please help me to get there.

DB: No, it is something different.

K: I know what you are saying.

Q: Can one see the illusory nature of that very demand that I want to go to heaven? Or I want to be enlightened, or I want to be this, I want to be that? But this very question, this very demand is . . .

K: This demand is based on becoming, on the more.

Q: That is illusory.

K: No. You say that.

DB: You haven't demonstrated it to me, you see.

K: That is an idea to you. It is just a theory. Show me.

Q: Well, are we willing really to explore the question?

K: We are willing on one condition — that we find something at the end of it. See how the human mind works. I will climb the highest mountain if I can get something out of it.

Q: Can the mind see that this is the problem?

K: Yes, but it can't let go.

Q: Well if it sees . . .

K: You are going round and round in circles!

DB: It sees the problem abstractly.

K: That is it. Now why do I see it abstractly?

DB: First of all, it is a lot easier.

K: Don't go back to that. Why does my mind make an abstraction of everything?

DB: Let's begin by saying that to a certain extent it is the function of thought to make abstractions outwardly, but then we carry them inwardly. It is the same sort of thing as before.

K: Yes. So is there something else — I am just asking — that we are missing in this altogether? That is, if I may point out, we are still thinking in the same old pattern.

DB: The question itself contains that pattern, doesn't it?

K: Yes, but the pursuit of the pattern is traditional.

DB: I mean that in framing this question, the pattern has continued.

K: Yes, so can we move away altogether from this, and look at it differently. Can the human mind say, all right, we have tried all this — Marx, Buddha, everybody has pointed out something or other. But obviously after a million years, we are still somehow caught in that pattern — saying we must be interested, we must listen, we must do this, and so on.

DB: That is still time.

K: Yes. Then what happens if I leave all that, *actually* leave it? I won't even think in terms of it. No more explanations, or new twists, that are the same old twists! So I say let's leave that area completely and look at the problem differently, the problem being, why do I always live in this centre of 'me'? I am a serious human being; I have listened to all this and after fifty years I know all the explanations — what I should, should not do, etc. Can I say, all right, I will discard all that? That means I stand completely alone. Does that lead anywhere?

DB: Possibly, yes.

K: I think it *does* lead somewhere.

DB: It seems to me that basically you are saying leave all this knowledge of mankind behind.

K: That is what I am saying.

DB: Apparently it is out of its place.

K: Yes. Leave all the knowledge, and experiences, explanations, causes that man has created — discard all that.

Q: But you are still left with the same mind.

K: Ah! I have not such a mind. It is *not* the same mind. When I discard all this, my mind has changed. My mind is *this*.

Q: No, isn't the mind also the basic set-up?

K: Which I have discarded.

Q: But you can't discard that.

K: Oh, yes.

Q: I mean this is an organism.

K: Now, wait a minute. My organism has been shaped by knowledge, by experience. And more knowledge which I have acquired as I have evolved, as I have grown. As I have gathered more and more, it has strengthened me, and I have been walking on that path for millenia. And I say, perhaps I may have to look at this problem totally differently — which is not to walk on that path at all, but to discard *all* knowledge I have acquired.

DB: In this area, in this psychological place.

K: Psychologically, of course.

DB: At the core, at the source, knowledge is irrelevant.

K: Yes.

DB: Further down the line it becomes relevant.

K: Of course. That is understood.

Q: But I have one question. The mind at the beginning of its evolution was in that same position. The mind at the beginning of whatever you call man was in that position.

K: No. I don't accept that. Why do you say that? The moment it comes into being, it is already caught in knowledge. Would you say that?

DB: I think it is implicit in the structure of thought.

K: That is just it.

DB: First of all, to have knowledge about the outward, and then to apply this to the inward, without understanding that it was going to be caught in it. Therefore it extended that knowledge into the area of psychological becoming.

Q: Well, if the mind started new, it would go through the same mistake again.

K: No, certainly not.

Q: Unless it has learnt.

K: No, I don't want to learn. You are still pursuing the same old path. I don't want to learn. Please, just let me go into this a little bit.

DB: We should clear this up because on other occasions you have said it is important to learn, even about observing yourself.

K: Of course.

DB: Now you are saying something quite different. It should be made clear why it is different. Why is it that you have given up the notion of learning at this stage?

K: At this stage, because I am still gathering memory.

DB: But there was a state when it was important to learn about the mind.

K: Don't go back. I am just starting. I have lived for sixty, eighty, or a hundred years. And I have listened to all this — the teachers in India, the Christians, the Muslims; I have listened to all the psychological explanations, to Freud, Marx and everybody.

DB: I think we should go a bit further. We agree that is all negative stuff, but in addition perhaps I have observed myself, and learned about myself.

K: Myself, yes, add that. And, at the end of it, I say perhaps this is a wrong way of looking at it.

DB: Right. Having explored that way, we finally are able to see it might be wrong.

K: Perhaps.

DB: Well I would say that in some sense perhaps it was necessary to explore that way.

K: Or not necessary.

DB: It may not have been, but given the whole set of conditions it was bound to happen.

K: Of course. So now I have come to a point when I say discard — we will put in that word — all that knowledge, because that hasn't led me anywhere, in the sense that I am not free of my egocentricism.

DB: But that alone isn't enough because if you say it hasn't worked, you can always hope or suppose that it *may*. But in fact you could see that it can't work.

K: It can't work. I am definite on that.

DB: It is not enough to say it hasn't worked, actually it *cannot* work.

K: It cannot work because it is based on time and knowledge, which is thought. And these explanations are based on thought — to acquire knowledge and so on and so on. Would you say that?

DB: As far as we have gone we have based them on knowledge and thought. And not only thought, but the habitual patterns of skill are an extension of thought.

K: So I put those aside, not casually, not with an interest in the future — but seeing the same pattern being repeated and repeated; different colours, different phrases, different pictures, different images — I discard all that totally. Instead of going North, as I have been going for millenia, I have stopped and am going East, which means my mind has changed.

DB: Has the structure of the 'me' gone?

K: Obviously.

DB: Without insight into it?

K: No. I won't bring in insight for the moment.

DB: But there was insight to do that. I mean to say that to consider doing it was an insight. The insight was the thing that worked.

K: I won't bring in that word.

DB: When you said that the whole thing could not work, I think that is an insight.

K: For me. I see it cannot work. But then we go back again to how do I acquire insight, and all that.

DB: But leaving that aside and just saying that it was an insight, the question of how to acquire it is not the point.

K: It is an insight that says 'out'.

Q: Out to the pattern.

K: No, finished with this constant becoming through experience, knowledge, patterns. Finished!

Q: Would you say that the kind of thinking afterwards, is a totally different kind of thinking? Evidently one still must think.

K: I am not sure.

Q: Well you may call it something else.

K: Ah, I won't call it anything else. Please I am just fishing around. After having lived a hundred years, I see everybody pointing out the way to end the self, and that way is based on thought, time, knowledge. And I say, sorry, I know all that, I have used that. I have an insight into that; therefore it falls away. Therefore the mind has broken the pattern completely. Not going North but East, you break the pattern.

Now, all right. Suppose Dr. Bohm has this insight, and has broken away from the pattern. Please let us help another human being to come to that. Don't say you must be interested, you must listen, then fall back — you follow? What is your communication with another human being, so that he hasn't got to go through all this mess? What will make me absorb so completely what you have said, so that it is in my blood, in my brain, *everything*, so that I see this thing? What will you do? Or is there nothing to do — you follow my question? Because if you have that insight it is a passion, it is not just a clever insight, nor is it possible to sit back and be comfortable; it is a *passion* that won't let you sit still, you must move, give — whatever it is. What will you do? You have that passion of this immense insight. And that passion must, like a river with a great volume of water flowing over the banks, move in the same way.

Now, I am a human being, ordinary, fairly intelligent, well read, experienced. I have tried this, that and the other thing, and I meet someone who is full of this, and I say, why won't I listen to him?

Q: I think we do listen.

K: Do we?

Q: Yes, I think so.

K: Just go very, very slowly. Do we so completely listen that there is no resistance, no saying why, what is the cause, why should I? You follow what I mean? We have been through all that. We have walked the area endlessly, back and forward from corner to corner, North, South, East, West. And 'X' comes along and says, look there is a different way of living, something totally new; which means listening *completely*.

Q: If there is a resistance one does not see the resistance.

K: Don't begin all over again on why you resist. I will show you your resistance, by talking. You know. But yet you go back.

Q: Krishnaji, did not your initial question go beyond this, when you asked, let's leave the listening, the rationality, the thought.

K: Yes, but that is just an idea. Will you *do* it? 'X' comes along and says, 'Look, eat this.'

Q: I would eat it if I could see it.

K: Oh, yes, you can see it, very clearly. We said, don't go back to the pattern. See! Then you say, how am I to see? which is the old pattern. Just see! 'X' refuses to enter that pattern.

Q: The pattern of explanation?

K: Knowledge, all that. He says come over, don't go back.

Q: Krishnaji, to talk about a normal situation in the world; there are a number of people who ask one with similar words to see, put thought aside; if one would really look at this thing one would see it. That is what the priests tell us. So what is the difference?

K: No, I am not a priest. I have left all that. I have left the church, the gods, Jesus, the Buddhas, the Krishnas, I have left all that, Marx, Engels, all the analysts, all the pundits, everybody. You see, you haven't done that. Ah, you say, no, I can't do it until you show me there is something else beyond all that. And 'X' says, 'Sorry.' Has that any meaning?

DB: Yes. I think that we say, leave all the knowledge behind. But knowledge takes many subtle forms which we don't see.

K: Of course. You are full of this insight and you have discarded all knowledge because of that. And another keeps on paddling over the pool of knowledge. And you say, leave it. The moment we enter into explanations we are back in the game. And you refuse to explain.

You see, explanations have been the boat in which to cross to the other shore. And the man on the other shore says there is no boat. But 'X' says, cross! He is asking something impossible, isn't he?

DB: If it doesn't happen right away, then it *is* impossible.

K: Absolutely. He is asking something impossible for one to do. I am meeting 'X', who is immovable. Either I have to go round him, avoid him or go over him. I can't do any of that. But 'X' won't leave me alone, in the sense that I have met something immovable. And it is there night and day with me. I can't battle with it because there is nothing to get hold of.

So what happens to me when I meet something that is completely solid, immovable, absolutely true, what happens to me? Is that the problem? That we have never met something like that? We may climb the Himalayas, but Everest is always there. In the same way, perhaps human beings have never met something irrevocable. Something absolutely immovable. Either we are terribly puzzled by it, or we say, well we can't do anything about it. Walk away from it. Or it is something that we must investigate — you follow — we must capture. Which is it?

Here is a solid thing. I am confronted by it. As I said, I might run away from it, which I generally do. Or worship it. Or try to understand what it is. When I do all these things, I am back in the old pattern. So I discard that. When meeting 'X', who is immovable, I see what the nature of it is. I am movable, as a human being, but 'X' is immovable. The contact with it does something, it must. It is not some mystic,.occult stuff but it is simple, isn't it?

Q: Sir, it functions like a magnet, but it doesn't break something.

K: No, because you haven't let go the pattern. It is not 'X's' fault.

Q: I didn't say it was.

K: No, the implication is that. Therefore you are back, you are dependent.

Q: What is taking place?

K: I am saying, you meet 'X'; what happens?

Q: You said, an effort to understand.

K: Ah, there you are, lost. You are back in the old pattern. You see it, you feel it, you know it, you recognize it. It doesn't matter what word you use, it is there.

DB: Well, can't you say that 'X' communicates the absolute necessity of not going on with the old pattern, because you see it absolutely can't work.

K: Yes, put it in your own words. All right.

DB: And therefore that is unalterable, immovable — is that what you mean?

K: Yes, I am movable; 'X' is immovable.

DB: Well, what is *behind* 'X', what is working in 'X' is immovable. Wouldn't you say that?

K: What is working is something of a shock at first, naturally. I have been moving, moving, moving, then I meet something that is immovable. Suddenly something takes place, obviously. You can see what takes place. 'X' is *not* becoming, and I am becoming. And 'X' has been through explanations and all the rest of it, and he shows that becoming is painful. (I am putting it quickly, in a few words.) And I meet that. So there is the sensitivity — all right, let's put it the other way. The explanations and the discarding of all the explanations have made me sensitive. Much more alert. When I meet something like 'X', naturally there is a response not in terms of explanation or understanding. There is a response to *that*. There is bound to be. Explanations have been given over and over again. I have listened, but either they have made me dull, or I begin to see that explanations have no value at all. So in this process I have become extraordinarily sensitive to any explanation. I am allergic!

There is a danger in this too, because, you know, people have said when you go to the guru he gives; so be silent and you will receive. That's an illusion, you know. Well, I have said enough.

DB: I could just say that when one sees that this whole process of time and knowledge and so on won't work, then it stops. Now, this leaves one more sensitive — right?

K: Yes, the mind has become sharp.

DB: All this movement was getting in the way.

K: Yes, psychological knowledge has made us dull.

DB: It has kept the brain moving in an unnecessary way.

Q: All knowledge?

DB: Well, no. You could say in some sense that knowledge needn't make you dull, I suppose, if it starts from the clarity of where we don't have this knowledge at the core . . .

K: Yes. You remember we said too, in our discussions, that the ground is not knowledge.

DB: You see the first thing is, it creates emptiness.

K: That's it.

DB: But not yet the ground, not immediately the ground.

K: That's right. You see, we have discussed all this; I hear it on the tape, it is printed in a book, and I say, yes I get it. By reading it, I have explained, I have acquired knowledge. Then I say, I must have that.

DB: The danger is that there is great difficulty in communicating this in a book because that is too fixed.

K: But that is what generally happens.

DB: But I think that the main point, which could communicate it, is to see that knowledge, in all its forms, subtle and obvious, cannot solve the psychological problem; it can only make it worse. But then there is another energy which is involved.

K: You see now what is happening? If any trouble arises I go to a psychologist. In any family trouble I go to somebody who will tell me what to do. Everything around me is being organized, and making me more and more helpless. That is what is happening.

10 APRIL 1980, OJAI, CALIFORNIA

FIVE

The Ground of Being, and the Mind of Man

———————————

DAVID BOHM: Perhaps we could go further into the nature of the ground; whether we could come to it and whether it has any relationship to human beings. And also whether there could be a change in the physical behaviour of the brain.

KRISHNAMURTI: Could we approach this question from the point of view, why do we have ideas? And is the ground an idea? That is where we must first be clear. Why have ideas become so important?

DB: Perhaps because the distinction between ideas, and what is beyond ideas, is not clear. Ideas are often taken to be something more than ideas; we feel they are not ideas but a reality.

K: That is what I want to find out. Is the ground an idea, or is it imagination, an illusion, a philosophic concept? Or something that is absolute, in the sense that there is nothing beyond it?

DB: How can you tell that there is nothing beyond it?

K: I am coming to that. I want to see whether we look at that, or perceive that, or have an insight into that, from a concept. Because after all the whole Western world — perhaps also the Eastern world — is based on concepts. The whole outlook and religious beliefs, are based on that. But do we approach it from that point of view or as a philosophic investigation — philosophic, in the sense, love of wisdom, love of truth, love of investigation, the process of the mind? Are we doing that when we discuss, when we want to investigate, explain, or find out what that ground is?

DB: Well, perhaps not all the philosophers have been basing their approach on concepts, although certainly philosophy is taught through concepts. Certainly it is very hard to teach it except through concepts.

K: What then is the difference between a religious mind and a philosophic mind? You understand what I am trying to convey?

Can we investigate the ground from a mind that is disciplined in knowledge?

DB: Fundamentally, inherently, we say that the ground is unknown. Therefore we can't begin with knowledge, and we have suggested we start with the unknown.

K: Yes. Say for instance 'X' says there is such a ground. And all of us, 'Y' and 'Z', say, what is that ground, prove it, show it, let it manifest itself? When we ask such questions, is it with a mind that is seeking, or rather that has this passion, this love for truth? Or are we merely saying let's talk about it?

DB: I think that in that mind there is the demand for certainty; we want to be *sure*. So there is no enquiring.

K: Suppose you state that there *is* such a thing, that there is the ground; it is immovable, etc. And I say, I want to find out. Show it, prove it to me. How can my mind, which has evolved through knowledge, which has been highly disciplined in knowledge, even touch that? Because *that* is not knowledge, it is not put together by thought.

DB: Yes, as soon as we say, prove it, we want to turn it into knowledge.

K: That's it!

DB: We want to be absolutely certain, so that there can be no doubt. And yet, on the other side of the coin, there is also the danger of self-deception and delusion.

K: Of course. The ground cannot be touched as long as there is any form of illusion, which is the projection of desire, pleasure or fear. So how do I perceive that thing? Is the ground an idea to be investigated? Or is it something that cannot be investigated?

DB: Right.

K: Because my mind is trained, disciplined, by experience and knowledge, and it can only function in that area. And someone comes along and tells me that this ground is not an idea, is not a philosophic concept; it is not something that can be put together, or perceived by thought.

DB: It cannot be experienced, it cannot be perceived or understood through thought.

K: So what have I? What am I to do? I have only this mind that has been conditioned by knowledge. How am I to move away from all that? How am I, an ordinary man, educated, well-read, experienced, to feel this thing, to touch it, to comprehend it?

You tell me words will not convey that. You tell me you must have a mind that is free from all knowledge, except that which is technological. And you are asking an impossible thing of me, aren't you? And, if I say I will make an effort, then that also is born out of the self-centred desire. So what shall I do? I think that is a very serious question. That is what every serious person asks.

DB: At least implicitly. They may not say it.

K: Yes, implicitly. So you, on the other side of the bank, as it were, tell me that there is no boat to cross in. You can't swim across. In fact you can't do anything. Basically, that is what it comes to. So what shall I do? You are asking me, you are asking the mind, not the general mind but . . .

DB: . . . the particular mind.

K: You are asking this particular mind to eschew all knowledge. Has this ever been said in the Christian or the Jewish worlds?

DB: I don't know about the Jewish world, but in some sense the Christians tell you to give your faith to God, to give over to Jesus, as the mediator between us and God.

K: Yes. Now Vedanta means the end of knowledge. And being a Westerner, I say, it means nothing to me. Because from the Greeks and all that, the culture in which I have lived has emphasized knowledge. But when you talk to some Eastern minds, they acknowledge in their religious life that a time must come when knowledge must end; the mind must be free of knowledge. Vedanta is the whole way of looking. But it is only a conceptual, a theoretical understanding. But to a Westerner, it means absolutely nothing.

DB: I think that there has been a Western tradition which is similar, but not as common. For example, in the Middle Ages there was a book called *The Cloud of Unknowing*, which is on that line, although it is not the main line of Western thought.

K: So what shall I do? How shall I approach the question? I want to find it. It gives meaning to life. It is not that my intellect gives meaning to life by inventing some illusion, some hope, some belief, but I see vaguely that this understanding, coming upon this ground, gives an immense significance to life.

DB: Well, people have used that notion of God to give significance to life.

K: No, no. God is merely an idea.

DB: Yes, but the idea contains something similar to the Eastern idea that God is beyond knowing. Most people accept it that way, though some may not. So there is some sort of similar notion.

K: But you tell me that the ground is not created by thought. So you cannot under any circumstances come upon it through any form of manipulation of thought.

DB: Yes, I understand. But I am trying to say that there is this problem, danger, delusion, in the sense that people say, 'Yes, that is quite true, it is through a direct experience of Jesus that we come upon it, not through the thought of God, you see!' I am not able to express their view accurately. Possibly, the grace of God?

K: The grace of God, yes.

DB: Something beyond thought, you see.

K: As a fairly educated, thoughtful man, I reject all that.

DB: Why do you reject it?

K: Because it has become common, first of all, common in the sense that everybody says that! And also there may be in it a great sense of illusion created by desire, hope, fear.

DB: Yes, but some people do seem to find this meaningful although it may be an illusion.

K: But if they had never heard of Jesus, they wouldn't experience Jesus.

DB: That seems reasonable.

K: They would experience something different that they have been taught. In India I mean . . .

QUESTIONER: But don't the more serious people in the religions say that essentially God, or whatever that is, the Absolute, the ground, is something that cannot be experienced through thinking? Also they might go so far as to say it cannot be experienced at all.

K: Oh, yes, I have said it cannot be experienced. 'X' says it cannot be experienced. Let's say, I don't know. Here is a person who says there *is* such a thing. And I listen to him, and not only does he convey it by his presence, but through the word. Although he tells me to be careful; the word is not the thing; but he uses the word to convey that there is this something so immense that my thought cannot capture it. And I say, all right, you have explained that very carefully, and how is my brain, that is conditioned, disciplined in knowledge, how is it to free itself from all that?

Q: Could it free itself by understanding its own limitation?

K: So you are *telling* me thought is limited. Show it to me! Not by talking or memory, experience or knowledge; I understand that, but I don't capture the feeling that it is limited, because I see the beauty of the earth, I see the beauty of a building, of a person, of nature. I see all that, but when you say thought is limited, I don't feel it. It is just a lot of words which you have said to me. Intellectually I understand. But I have no feeling for it. There is no perfume in it. How will you show me — not show me — how will you help me — not help — aid me, to have this feeling that thought itself is brittle, it is such a small affair? So that it is in my blood — you understand? When once it is in my blood, I have got it. You don't have to explain it.

Q: But isn't that the possible approach, not to talk about the ground, that at the moment is far too removed, but rather to look directly at what the mind can do.

K: Which is thinking.

Q: The mind is thinking.

K: That is all I have. Thinking, feeling, hating, loving — you know all that. The activity of the mind.

Q: Well, I would say we don't know it, we only think we know it.

K: I know when I am angry. I know when I am wounded. It is not an idea, I have got the feeling, I am carrying the hurt inside me. I am fed up with the investigation because I have done it all my life. I go to Hinduism, Buddhism, Christianity, Islam — and I say I have investigated, studied, looked at them. I say these are all just words. How do I as a human being have this extraordinary feeling about it? If I have no passion, I am not investigating. I want to have this passion that will explode me out of this little enclosure. I have built a wall around myself, a wall, which is myself. And man has lived with this thing for millions of years. And I have been trying to get out of it by studying, by reading, by going to gurus, by all kinds of things, but I am still anchored there. And you talk about the ground, because you see something that is breath-taking, that seems so alive, so extraordinary. And I am here, anchored in here. You, who have 'seen' the ground, must do something that will explode, break up this centre completely.

Q: *I* must do something, or *you* must?

K: Help me! Not by prayer, and all that nonsense. You understand what I am trying to say? I have fasted, I have meditated, I have renounced, I have taken a vow of this and that. I have done all those things. Because I have had a million years of life. And at the end of the million years I am still where I was, at the beginning. This is a great discovery for me; I thought I had moved on from the beginning, by going through all this, but I suddenly discover I am back at the same point where I started. I have had more experience, I have seen the world, I have painted, I have played music, I have danced — you follow? But I have come back to the original starting point.

Q: Which is me and not me.

K: *Me.* I say to myself, what am I to do? And what is the human mind's relationship to the ground? Perhaps if I could establish a relationship it might break up this centre, totally. This is not a motive, not a desire, not a reward. I see that if the mind could establish a relationship with *that*, my mind has become that — right?

Q: But hasn't mind then already become that?

K: Oh, no.

Q: But I think you have just wiped away the greatest difficulty in saying there is no desire.

K: No, no. I said I have lived a million years . . .

Q: But that is an insight.

K: No. I won't accept insight so easily as that.

Q: Well, let me put it this way: it is something much more than knowledge.

K: No, you are missing my point. My brain has lived for a million years. It has experienced everything. It has been Buddhist, Hindu, Christian, Muslim; it has been all kinds of things, but the core of it is the same. And someone comes along and says, look there is a ground which is . . . something! Am I going back to what I have already known — the religions, etc.? I reject all that, because I say I have been through it all, and they are like ashes to me at the end of it.

DB: Well, all those things were the attempt to create an apparent ground by thought. It seemed that through knowledge and thought, people created what they regarded as the ground. And it wasn't.

K: It wasn't. Because man has spent a million years at it.

DB: So long as knowledge enters the ground, that will be false?

K: Of course. So is there a relationship between that ground and the human mind? In asking that question, I am also aware of the danger of such a question.

DB: Well, you may create a delusion of the same kind that we have already gone through.

K: Yes. I have played that song before.

Q: Are you suggesting that the relationship cannot be made by you, but it must come . . . ?

K: I am asking that. No, it may be that I have to make a relationship. My mind now is in such a state that I won't accept a thing. My mind says I have been through all this before. I have suffered, I have searched, I have looked, I have investigated, I have lived with people who are awfully clever at this kind of thing.

So I am asking the question, being fully aware of the danger of it, as when the Hindus say, God is in you, Brahman is in you — which is a lovely idea! But I have been through all that.

So I am asking if the human mind has no relationship to the ground, and if there is only a one-way passage, from that to me . . .

DB: Surely that's like the grace of God then, that you have invented.

K: That I won't accept.

DB: You are not saying the relationship *is* one way, nor are you saying it is *not* one way.

K: Maybe; I don't know.

DB: You are not saying anything.

K: I am not saying anything. All that I 'want' is this centre to be blasted. You understand? For the centre not to exist. Because I see that the centre is the cause of all the mischief, all the neurotic conclusions, all the illusions, all the endeavour, all the effort, all the misery — *everything* is from that core. After a million years, I haven't been able to get rid of it; it hasn't gone. So is there a relationship at all? What is the relationship between goodness and evil? Consider it. There is no relationship.

DB: It depends on what you mean by relationship.

K: Contact, touch, communication, being in the same room . . .

DB: . . . coming from the same root.

K: Yes.

Q: But are we then saying that there is the good, and there is the evil?

K: No, no. Let's use another word; whole, and that which is not whole. It is not an *idea*. Now is there relationship between these two? Obviously not.

DB: No, if you are saying that in some sense the centre is an illusion. An illusion cannot be related to that which is true, because the content of the illusion has no relation to what is true.

K: That's it. You see, that is a great discovery. I want to establish relationship with that. 'Want'; I am using rapid words to convey something. This petty little thing wants to have relationship with that immensity. It cannot.

DB: Yes, not just because of its immensity, but because in fact this thing is not — actually?

K: Yes.

Q: But I don't see that. He says the centre is not actual, but I don't see that the centre is not actual.

DB: Not actual, in the sense of not being genuine but an illusion. I mean, something is acting but it is not the content which we know.

K: Do you see that?

Q: You say the centre must explode. It does not explode because I don't see the falseness in it.

K: No. You have missed my point. I have lived a million years, I have done all this. And at the end of it I am still back at the beginning.

Q: So you say the centre must explode.

K: No, no, no. The mind says this is too terribly small. And it can't do anything about it. . . . It has prayed, it has done everything. But the centre is still there. And someone tells me there is this ground. I want to establish a relationship with that.

Q: He tells me there is this thing, and also says that the centre is an illusion.

DB: Wait, that is too quick.

K: No. Wait. I know it is there. Call it what you like, an illusion, a reality, a fiction — whatever you like. It is there. And the mind says, it is not good enough; it wants to capture *that*. It wants to have relationship with it. And *that* says, 'Sorry, you can't have relationship with me.' That's all!

Q: Is that mind which wants to be in connection, in relationship with that, the same mind which is the 'me'?

K: Don't split it up, please. You are missing something. I have lived all this. I know, I can argue with you, back and forth. I have a million years of experience, and it has given me a certain capacity. And I realize at the end of it all there is no relationship between me and truth. And that's a tremendous shock to me. It is as if you have knocked me out, because my million years of experience say, go after that, seek it, pray for it, struggle for it, cry, sacrifice for it. I have done all that. And suddenly it is pointed out that I cannot have relationship with that. I have shed tears, left my family, *everything*, for that. And *that* says, 'No relationship'. So what has happened to me? This is what I want to get at. Do you understand what I am saying — what has happened to me? To the mind that has lived this way, done everything in search of that, when that says, 'You have no relationship with me'. This is the greatest thing . . .

Q: It is a tremendous shock to the 'me', if you say that.

K: Is it to you?

Q: I think it was, and then . . .

K: Don't! I am asking you, is it a shock to discover that your brain, and your mind, your knowledge, are valueless? All your examinations, all your struggles, all the things that you have gathered through years and years, centuries, are absolutely worthless? Do you go mad, because you say you have done all this for nothing? Virtue, abstinence, control, everything — and at the end of it, you say they are valueless! Do you understand what this does to you?

DB: I mean, if the whole thing goes, then it is of no consequence.

K: Absolutely, you have no relationship. What you have done or not done is absolutely of no value.

DB: Not in any fundamental sense. It has relative value, relative value only within a certain framework, which in itself has no value.

K: Yes, thought has relative value.

DB: But the framework in general has no value.

K: That's right. The ground says, whatever you have done 'on earth' has no meaning. Is that an idea? Or an actuality? Idea being that you have told me, but I still go on, struggling, wanting, groping. Or is it an actuality, in the sense that I suddenly realize the futility of *all* that I have done. So, one must be very careful to see that it is not a concept; or rather that one doesn't translate it into a concept or an idea, but receive the full blow of it!

Q: You see, Krishnaji, for hundreds of years, probably since man has existed, he has pursued what he calls God, or the ground.

K: As an idea.

Q: But then the scientific mind came along, and also said it is just an idea, it is just foolish.

K: Oh, no! The scientific mind says that through investigating matter we will perhaps come upon the ground.

DB: Yes, many feel that way. Some would even add, investigate the brain, you see.

K: Yes. That is the purpose of investigating the mind, not to blast each other off the earth, with guns. We are talking of 'good' scientists, not governmental scientists, but those who say, we are examining matter, the brain and all that, to find out if there is something beyond all this.

Q: And many people, many scientists, would say that they have found the ground; the ground is empty, it is emptiness; it is an energy which is different from man.

K: Now, is that an idea, or an actuality to them, which affects their life, their blood, their mind, their relationship with the world?

Q: I think it is just an idea.

K: Then I am sorry, I have been through that. I was a scientist ten thousand years ago! You follow? I have been through all that. If it is merely an idea, we can both play at that game. I can send the ball to you, it is in your court, and you can send it back to me. We can play that. But I have finished with that kind of game.

DB: Because, in general, what people discover about matter does not seem to affect them deeply, psychologically

K: No, of course not.

DB: You might think that if they saw the whole unity of the universe they would act differently, but they don't.

Q: You could say that it has affected some of their lives. You see the whole Communist doctrine is built on the idea (which they think is a fact) that whatever is, is just a material process, which is essentially empty. So then man has to organize his life and society according to those dialectical principles.

K: No, no, dialectical principles are opinion opposing another opinion; man hoping, out of opinions, to find the truth.

DB: I think we should leave this aside. There are ways of looking at different meanings of the word dialectical — but one needs to see reality as a flowing movement; not to see things as fixed, but to see them in movement and interconnection. I think that you could say that whatever way people managed to look at it, after they saw this unity it didn't fundamentally change their lives. In Russia, the same structures of the mind, if not worse, hold as elsewhere. And wherever people have tried this, it has not actually, fundamentally, affected the way they feel and think, and the way they live.

Q: You see, what I wanted to say is that the dismissal of the pursuit of the ground has not had any shocking effect on people.

K: No! I am not interested. It has given me a tremendous shock to discover the truth, that all the churches, prayers, books, have absolutely no meaning — except how we can build a better society, and so on.

DB: If we could manage to bring this point to order, then it would have great meaning — to build a good society. But as long as this disorder is at the centre, we can't use that in the right way. I think it would be more accurate to say that there is a great *potential* meaning in all that. But it does not affect the centre, and there is no sign that it has ever done so.

Q: You see what I don't understand is that there are many people who in their life have never pursued what you call the ground.

K: They are not interested.

Q: Well, I am not so sure. How would you approach such a person?

K: I am not interested in approaching any person. All the works I have done — everything I have done — the ground says are valueless. And if I can drop all that, my mind is the ground. Then from there I move. From *there* I create society.

DB: I think you could say that as long as you are looking for the ground somewhere by means of knowledge, then you are getting in the way.

K: So to come back to earth; why has man done this?

DB: Done what?

K: Accumulated knowledge. Apart from the necessity of having factual knowledge in certain areas, why has this burden of knowledge continued for so long?

DB: Because in one sense man has been trying to produce a solid ground through knowledge. Knowledge has tried to create a ground. That is one of the things that has happened.

K: Which means what?

DB: It means illusion again.

K: Which means that the saints, the philosophers, have educated me — in knowledge and through knowledge — to find the ground.

Q: To create a ground. You see, in a way, there used to be all these periods when mankind was caught in superstition. And knowledge was able to do away with that.

K: Oh, no.

Q: To some extent it was.

K: Knowledge has only crippled me from seeing truth. I stick to that. It hasn't cleared me of my illusions. Knowledge may be illusory itself.

Q: That may be, but it has cleared up some illusions.

K: I want to clear up *all* the illusions that I hold — not some. I have got rid of my illusion about nationalism; I have got rid of illusion about belief, about this, about that. At the end of it, I realize my mind is illusion. You see, to me, who have lived for a thousand years, to find all this is absolutely worthless, is something enormous.

DB: When you say you have lived for a thousand years, or a million years, does that mean, in a sense, that all the experience of mankind is . . . ?

K: . . . is me.

DB: . . . is me. Do you feel that?

K: I do.

DB: And how do you feel it?

K: How do we feel anything? Wait a minute, I will tell you. It is not sympathy, or empathy, it is not a thing that I have desired, it is a *fact*, an absolute, irrevocable fact.

DB: Could we share that feeling, perhaps? You see, that seems to be one of the steps that is missing, because you have repeated that quite often as an important part of the whole thing.

K: Which means that when you love somebody there is no 'me' — it is love. In the same way, when I say I am humanity, it is so; it is not an idea, it is not a conclusion, it is part of me.

DB: Let's say it is a feeling that I have gone through all that, all that you describe.

K: Human beings have been through all that.

DB: If others have gone through it, then I also have gone through it.

K: Of course. One is not aware of it.

DB: No, we separate.

K: If we admit that our brains are not my particular brain, but the brain that has evolved through millenia . . .

DB: Let me say why this doesn't communicate so easily: everybody feels that the content of his brain is in some way individual, that *he* hasn't gone through all that. Let's say that somebody, thousands of years ago, went through science or philosophy. Now how does that affect me? That is what is not clear.

K: Because I am caught in this self-centred, narrow little cell, which refuses to look beyond. But you as a scientist, as a religious man, come along and tell me that your brain is the brain of mankind.

DB: Yes, and all knowledge is the knowledge of mankind. So that in some way we have all knowledge.

K: Of course.

DB: Though not in detail.

K: So you tell me that, and I understand what you mean, not verbally, not intellectually; it is so. But I come to that only when I have given up ordinary things, like nationality, etc.

DB: Yes, we have given up the divisions, and we can see that the experience is of all mankind.

K: It is so obvious. You go to the most primitive village in India, and the peasant will tell you all about his problems, his wife, children, poverty. It is exactly the same thing, only he is wearing different clothes or whatever! For 'X', this is an indisputable fact; it is so. He says, all right, at the end of all this, of all these years, I suddenly discover that it is empty. You see, we don't accept it, we are too clever. We are so soaked with disputations and arguments and knowledge. We don't see a simple fact. We refuse to see it. And 'X' comes along and says, see it, it is there: then the immediate machinery of thought begins — and says, be silent. So I practise silence! I have done that for a thousand years. It has led nowhere.

So there is only one thing, and that is to discover that *all* that I have done is useless — ashes! You see that doesn't depress one. That is the beauty of it. I think it is like the Phoenix.

DB: Rising from the ashes.

K: Born of ashes.

DB: In a way it is freedom, to be free of all that.

K: Something totally new is born.

DB: Now what you said before is that the mind is the ground, it is the unknown.

K: The mind? Yes. But not this mind.

DB: In that case it is not the same mind.

K: If I have been through all that, and come to a point when I have to end all that, it is a new mind.

DB: That's clear, the mind is its content, and the content is knowledge, and without that knowledge it is a new mind.

12 APRIL 1980, OJAI, CALIFORNIA

SIX

Can Insight Bring About a Mutation of the Brain Cells?

DAVID BOHM: You have said that insight changes the brain cells, and I wonder if we could discuss that?

KRISHNAMURTI: As it is constituted, the brain functions in one direction: memory, experience, knowledge. It has functioned in that area as much as possible, and most people are satisfied with it.

DB: Well, they don't know of anything else.

K: And also they have placed knowledge in supreme import- ance. If one is concerned with fundamental change, where does one begin? Suppose 'X' feels he will go along a certain direction set by mankind. He has been going there century after century, and he asks himself what is radical change; if it is in the environment, or in human relationships; if it is a sense of love, which is not in the area of knowledge. Where is it to begin? You understand my question? Unless there is some mutation taking place inside here, inside my mind, the brain, I may *think* I have changed, but it is a superficial change, and not a change in depth.

DB: Yes. What is implied there is that the present state of affairs involves not only the mind but also the nervous system and the body. Everything is set in a certain way.

K: Of course. That is what I meant, the whole movement is set in a certain way. And along that pattern I can modify, adjust, polish a little more, a little less and so on. But if a man is concerned with radical change, where is he to begin? As we said the other day, we have relied on the environment or society and various disciplines to change us, but I feel these are all in the same direction.

DB: In so far as they all emanate from this thing, the way the mind and body are set, they are not going to change anything. There is a total structure involved which is in the brain, in the body, in the whole of society.

K: Yes, yes. So what am I to do? What is 'X' to do? And in asking this question, what is there to change?

DB: What exactly do you mean by 'what is there to change'? What is to be changed?

K: Yes, both; what is there to be changed, and what is there to change? Basically, what is there to change? 'X' sees that he can change certain things along this way, but to go much further than that, what is one to do? I am sure man has asked this question. You must have asked it. But apparently the mutation hasn't taken place. So what is 'X' to do? He realizes the need for a radical revolution, a psychological revolution; he perceives that the more he changes, it is the same thing continuing; the more he enquires into himself, the enquiry remains the same, and so on. So what is there to change; unless 'X' finds a way to change the brain itself?

DB: But what will change the brain?

K: That's it. The brain has been set in a pattern for millenia! I think it is no longer 'what' should I change. It is imperative that I change.

DB: So it is agreed that there must be a change, but the question is still, how can the brain change?

K: One must come to that point. If this question is put to you as a scientist, or as a human being who is involved in science, what would your answer be?

DB: I don't think science can deal with it, because it doesn't go far enough. It can't possibly probe that deeply into the structure of the brain. Many questions are positing the relationship of brain and mind, which science has not been able to resolve. Some people would say that there is nothing beyond the brain. . . .

K: . . . Purely materialistic; I understand all that.

DB: If it is not materialistic, then for the moment science has very little to say about it. Perhaps some people would try to, but science generally has been most successful, most systematic, in dealing with matter. Any attempt to do otherwise is not very clear.

K: So you would tell 'X', to change inside in the brain cells, etc. My immediate answer to that is, how? Everybody asks that. It is not a matter of faith. It is not a matter of changing one pattern to another pattern. So you leave me without any direction — right? You leave me without any instrument that can penetrate this.

DB: Except that you are implying there is something beyond the brain, in putting that question. We don't *know*. The very statement implies that insight is somehow beyond the brain, else it couldn't change the brain.

K: Yes. So how am I to capture it? Maybe I can't capture it . . .

DB: . . . but how will it come about? You are saying that something that is non-material can affect matter. This is the implication.

K: I am not sure.

DB: I think that clearing this up, would make more clear what your question is. It is somewhat puzzling if you don't.

K: All that you have said to me is, insight changes, brings about mutation in the brain. Now you explain what insight is, which is not a result of a progressive knowledge, not progressive time, not a remembrance. This insight may be the real activity of the brain.

DB: All right. Let's put it differently. The brain has many activities which include memory, and all these that you have mentioned. In addition there is a more inward activity, but it is still the activity of the brain.

K: It may be the same.

DB: You see, in putting this, something seems to be not quite clear.

K: Yes. We must be very clear that it is not the result of progressive knowledge; it is not come by through any exercise of will.

DB: Agreed. I think people can generally see that insight comes in a flash, it does not come through will. Those who have considered it at all can see that. Also, that chemistry will probably not bring it about.

K: I think most people who are concerned see that. But how am I, as 'X', to have this insight? I see your logic, I see your reason.

DB: In some ways it may disturb people. It is not clear what the logic is, what is going to make this change in the brain. Is it something more than the brain, or is it something deeper *in* the brain? This is one of the questions.

K: Of course.

DB: It is not quite clear logically.

QUESTIONER: Are you saying that there is a function of the brain which acts without reference to its content?

K: Yes, to the past, to the content.

DB: This is a good question. Is there a function in the brain which is independent of the content? Which is not conditioned by the content, but that might still be a physical function?

K: I understand. Is this the question? Apart from the consciousness with its content, is there in the brain an activity which is not touched by consciousness?

DB: By the content; yes.

K: Content *is* the consciousness.

DB: Yes, but sometimes we use the word in another sense. Sometimes we imply that there could be another kind of consciousness. So if we call it 'content' it would be more clear.

K: All right. A part of the brain which is not touched by the content.

DB: Yes, this suggests that it may be possible for the brain to change. Either the brain is entirely controlled by its content, or in some way it is not conditioned.

K: That is a dangerous concept!

DB: But it is what you are saying.

K: No. See the danger of it. See the danger of admitting to oneself that there is a part of the brain . . .

DB: . . . an activity . . .

K: . . . all right, an activity of the brain which is not touched by the content.

DB: It is a possible activity. It may be that it has not been awakened.

K: It has not been awakened. That's right.

Q: But what is the danger?

K: That is simple enough. The danger is that I am admitting there is God in me, that there is something super-human; something beyond the content which therefore will operate on it, or that will operate in spite of it.

Q: But which part of the brain sees the danger?

K: Let us go slowly. Which part of the brain sees the danger? Of course it is the content that sees the danger.

Q: Does it?

K: Oh, yes, because the content is aware of all the tricks it has played.

DB: This is similar to many of the old tricks.

K: Yes.

DB: Those tricks we have discussed before — the assumption of God within, the imagination of God within. There is a danger here obviously.

Q: But could the brain, seeing the danger, make that statement nevertheless? Because that statement might be pointing to the right direction.

DB: Even though it is dangerous, it may be necessary to do so; it may be on the right track.

K: The unconscious, which is part of the content, may capture this, and say, 'Yes' — so it sees the danger instantly.

Q: It sees its own trap.

K: Yes, it sees the trap which it has created. So it avoids that trap. That is sanity: to avoid a trap is sanity. Is there an activity which is totally independent of the content? Then, is that activity part of the brain?

DB: Is it a natural activity of the brain? Material in the brain.

K: Which means what?

DB: Well, if there is such a natural activity, it could awaken somehow, and that activity could change the brain.

K: But would you say it is still material?

DB: Yes. There could be different levels of matter, you see.

K: That is what I am trying to get at. Right.

DB: But you see, if you think that way, there could be a deeper level of matter which is not conditioned by the content. For example, we know matter in the universe is not conditioned by the content of our brains generally. There could be a deeper level of matter not conditioned in that way.

K: So it would still be matter, refined, or 'super', or whatever; it would still be the content.

DB: Why do you say that? You see, you have to go slowly. Do you say that matter is content?

K: Yes.

DB: Inherently? But this has to be made clear, because it is not obvious.

K: Let's discuss it. Let's grip this. Thought is matter.

DB: Well, thought is part of the content, part of the material process. Whether it exists independently as matter is not so clear. You can say, water is matter; you can pour water from one glass to another, it has an independent substance. But it is not clear whether thought could stand as matter by itself, except with some other material substance like the brain in which it takes place. Is that clear?

K: I don't quite follow.

DB: If you say water is matter, then it is clear. Now if you say, thought is matter, then thought must have a similar independent substance. You say air is matter — right? Or water is matter. Now waves are not matter, they are just a process in matter. Is it clear what I mean?

K: Yes. A wave is a process in matter.

DB: A material process. Is thought matter, or is it a process in matter?

Q: May one ask, is electricity considered to be matter?

DB: In so far as there are electron particles it is matter, but it is also a movement of that, which is a process.

Q: So it is two things.

DB: Well you can form waves of electricity, and so on.

Q: Waves would be the matter, but not the electrical action.

DB: The electrical action is like the waves, but the electricity consists of particles.

K: What is the question we are now asking?

DB: Is thought a material substance, or is it a process in some other material substance — like the brain?

K: It is a material process in the brain.

DB: Yes, scientists would generally agree with that.

K: Let's stick to that.

DB: If you say it is matter, they would become very puzzled.

K: I see.

Q: It doesn't exist apart from the brain cells. It resides in the brain.

K: That is, thought is a material process in the brain. That would be right. Then can that material process ever be independent?

DB: Independent of what?

K: Independent of something that is *not* a material process. No, wait a minute, we must go slowly. Thought is a material process in the brain. We all agree about this?

DB: Yes, you would get very wide agreement on that.

K: Then our question is, can that material process in the brain bring about a change in itself?

DB: Yes, that is the question.

K: In itself. And if that material in itself can change, it would still be a material process. Right?

DB: Yes. Thought is always apparently going to be a material process.

K: And therefore it is not insight. We must come back to that.

DB: You are saying that insight is not a material process?

K: Go slowly. We must be careful in using words. Thought is a material process in the brain; and any other movement, springing from that material process, is still material.

DB: Yes, it has to be.

K: Right. Is there another activity which is not a material process?

DB: Of course people have asked that question for ages. Is there spirit beyond matter?

K: Spirit, Holy Ghost! Is there some other activity of the brain which cannot be related to the material process?

DB: Well, it cannot depend upon it. Insight cannot depend on the material process, as it would then be just another material process.

K: Insight cannot depend on the material process, which is thought.

DB: But you were putting it the other way round, that the material process may depend on insight, may be changed by insight.

K: Ah, wait. The material process is dependent on it, but insight is *not* dependent on that process.

DB: Now many people would not see how something non-material would affect something material.

K: Yes, quite.

DB: It might be easily agreed that something non-material is not affected by matter, but then how does the operation work the other way?

K: What do you say? The brain, thought, with its content, is a material process. *Any* activity from it is still part of that. Now is insight part of that too?

DB: We have agreed on its independence of that; it can't be part of it. But it can still act within the material process, that's the crucial thing.

K: Yes. That's right. Insight is independent of the material process, but yet it can act upon it.

DB: Let's discuss that a little. Generally speaking, in science, if 'A' can act on 'B' there is usually reciprocal action of 'B' on 'A'. We don't find situations where 'A' acts on 'B', but 'B' never acts on 'A'.

K: I see, I see.

DB: This is one of the difficulties you have raised. We don't find this elsewhere; in human relations, if I can act on you, you can act on me — right?

K: Yes, we see that human relationships are interaction.

DB: Yes, mutual relationships.

K: And in those relationships there is response, and so on. Now, if I don't respond to your action, I am independent of it.

DB: But you see, science generally finds that it is not possible to have a one-sided action.

K: Quite. So we are continually insisting that the material process must have a relationship to the other.

DB: An action, anyway. Relationship is an ambiguous word here. If you said action it would be more clear.

K: All right. The material process must be able to act on the non-material, and the non-material must act on the material.

DB: But that would make them both the same.

K: Exactly!

Q: Not necessarily. One could envisage that insight is a much larger movement than the material process of the brain, and therefore that the larger movement can act on the smaller movement, but the smaller cannot act on the larger.

K: Yes, we are saying the same thing.

DB: The small movement has no significant action on the larger movement. You can have a situation that if you drop a rock in the ocean, the ocean absorbs it with no significant change.

K: Yes.

Q: So then they would still have a two-way action but only one action would be significant.

K: No, no. Don't enter into that too quickly, let us be careful. Love has no relationship to hate.

DB: Again there is this word 'relationship'. Would you, for example, say that hate has no action on love?

K: They are independent.

DB: Independent, they have no action on each other.

K: Ah, it is a very important thing to discover this. Love is independent of hate. Where there is hate the other cannot exist.

DB: Yes, they can't stand side by side, acting on each other.

K: They can't. So when scientists say, if 'A' has a relationship to 'B', then 'B' must have a relationship to 'A', we are contradicting that.

DB: Not *all* scientists have said that; a few have said otherwise — I don't like to bring in Aristotle . . .

K: Bring him in!

DB: He said there is an unmoved mover, that God is never moved by matter; he is not acted on by matter, but he acts. Do you see? That is an old idea then. Since Aristotle's time, science has thrown out this concept, and said that it is impossible.

K: If I see clearly that love is independent of hate, hate cannot possibly act on love. Love may act on hate, but where hate is, the other cannot be.

DB: Well, those are two possibilities. Which are you saying?

K: What are the two possibilities?

DB: You said, one possibility is that love may act on hate, and the other is that they have no action at all on each other.

K: Yes.

DB: But which?

K: I understand. No, love cannot act on hate.

DB: Right. They have no relationship. But perhaps insight could, you see.

K: We have to be quite clear on this point. Violence, and being without violence, are two entirely different factors. One cannot act upon the other.

DB: In that case you could say that the existence of the one is the non-existence of the other, and there is no way in which they can act together.

K: That's right.

DB: They cannot be there together.

K: Absolutely. I'll stick to that. So when this material process is in action, the other cannot exist.

DB: What is 'the other' this time? Insight?

K: Yes.

DB: That denies what we were saying before; that there is an action from insight on the material process.

K: Now, steady, yes. Where there is violence the other — I hate to use the word 'non-violence' — is not.

DB: Peace, or harmony?

K: Where there is violence, peace cannot exist. But where there is peace, is there violence? No, of course not. So peace is independent of violence.

Q: You have said many, many times that intelligence can act upon thought; insight can affect thought, but it doesn't work the other way round. You have given many examples of this.

K: Intelligence can wipe away ignorance, but ignorance cannot touch intelligence — right? Where there is love, hate can never exist. Can love wipe away hate?

DB: We said that this doesn't seem to be possible, because hate appears to be an independent force.

K: Of course it is.

DB: It has its own momentum, you see, its own force, its own movement.

Q: I don't quite get this relationship of love and hate with the earlier discussion of insight.

DB: There seem to be two different areas.

Q: Thought is a movement, and insight seems to be non-movement, where everything seemingly is at rest, and it can observe movement.

DB: That is what we are trying to get at, the notion of something which is not affected by anything else.

Q: Aren't you then saying, in looking at love and hate, that there is good and there is evil, and that evil is a completely separate, independent force?

DB: Well, it is independent of good.

Q: But is the process in the mind, or is it related to insight?

DB: We are coming to that.

Q: Take light and darkness. Light appears, and the darkness is gone.

DB: Good and evil; love and hate; light and darkness — when one is, the other can't be, you see. That is all we are saying so far.

Q: Do you mean, in a single brain?

DB: In any brain, yes, or in any group, or anywhere. Whenever there is hate going on in a group, there is not love.

K: Something has just come to my mind. Love has no cause. Hate has a cause. Insight has no cause. The material process, as thought, has a cause. Right?

DB: Yes, it is part of the chain of cause and effect.

K: Can that which has no cause ever act upon that which has a cause?

DB: It might. We can see no reason why that which has no cause might not act on something that has a cause. There is no obvious reason. It won't happen the other way round. What has a cause cannot act on that, which has no cause, because that would invalidate it.

K: That's right. But apparently the action of insight has an extraordinary effect on the material process.

DB: It may for example wipe out some causes.

K: As insight is causeless, it has a definite effect on that which has cause.

DB: Well, it doesn't necessarily follow, but it is possible.

K: No, no, I don't say it is possible.

DB: I am saying we haven't quite seen why it is necessary. There is no contradiction when we say the word possible.

K: All right, I see. As long as we are clear on the word possible. We must be careful. Love is without cause, and hate has a cause. The two cannot co-exist.

DB: Yes. That is true. That is why there is a difference between love and insight. That is why it doesn't follow necessarily that if something has no cause it will act on something that has a cause. That is what I was trying to say.

K: I just want to explore a little more. Is love insight?

DB: As far as we can see it is not the same. Love and insight are not identical, are they? Not exactly the same thing.

K: Why?

DB: Insight may be love, but, you see, insight also occurs in a flash.

K: It is a flash of course. And that flash alters the whole pattern, operates on it, uses the pattern, in the sense that I argue, reason, use logic, and all that. I don't know if I am making myself clear?

DB: I think that once the flash has operated, the pattern is different, and would therefore be more rational. The flash may make logic possible, because you may have been confused before the flash.

K: Yes, yes! Aristotle may have come to all this by logic.

DB: Well, he may have had some insight! We don't know.

K: We don't know, but I am questioning it.

DB: We really don't know how his mind operated because there are only a few books that have survived.

K: Would you say by reading some of those books that he had insight?

DB: I haven't really read Aristotle directly; very few people have because it is hard. Most people read what other people have said about Aristotle. A few phrases of his are common, like 'the unmoved mover'. And he has said some things which suggest that he was quite intelligent, at least.

K: What I am trying to say is that insight is never partial; I am talking of total, not partial, insight.

Q: Krishnaji, could you explain that a little? What do you mean by 'not partial' insight?

K: An artist can have a partial insight. A scientist can have a partial insight. But we are talking about total insight.

Q: You see the artist is also a human being, so . . .

K: But his capture of insight is partial.

Q: It is directed to some form of art. So you mean that it illuminates a limited area, or subject. Is that what you mean by partial insight?

K: Yes.

Q: Then what would be total insight? What would it encompass?

K: The total human activity.

DB: That is one point. But earlier on, we were asking whether this insight would illuminate the brain, the activity of the brain. In that illumination, it seems that the material activity of the brain will change. Would that be correct? We must get this point clear, then we can raise the question of totality. Are we saying that insight is an energy which illuminates the activity of the brain? And that in this illumination, the brain itself begins to act differently.

K: You are quite right. That's all. That is what takes place. Yes.

DB: We say the source of this illumination is not in the material process; it has no cause.

K: No cause.

DB: But it is a real energy.

K: It is pure energy. Is there action without cause?

DB: Yes, without time. Cause implies time.

K: That is, this flash has altered completely the pattern which the material process has set.

DB: Could you say that the material process generally operates in a kind of darkness, and therefore it has set itself on a wrong path?

K: In darkness, yes. That is clear. The material process acts in ignorance, in darkness. And this flash of insight enlightens the whole field, which means that ignorance and darkness have been dispelled. I will hold to that.

DB: You could say, then, that darkness and light cannot co-exist for obvious reasons. Nevertheless the very existence of light is to change the process of darkness.

K: Quite right.

Q: But what contributes the flash?

K: We haven't come to that yet. I want to go step by step into this. What has happened is that the material process has worked in darkness, and has brought about confusion, and all the mess that exists in the world. But this flash of insight wipes away the darkness. Which means that the material process is not then working in darkness.

DB: Right. But now let's make another point clear. When the flash has gone, the light continues.

K: The light is there, the flash is the light.

DB: At a certain moment the flash is immediate, but then, as you work from there, there is still light.

K: Why do you differentiate flash from light?

DB: Simply because the word 'flash' suggests something that happens in one moment.

K: Yes.

DB: You see, we are saying that insight would only last in that moment.

K: We must go slowly.

DB: Well, it is a matter of language.

K: Is it merely a matter of language?

DB: Perhaps not, but if you use the word 'flash', there is the analogy of lightning, giving light for a moment, but then the next moment you are in darkness, until there is a further flash of lightning.

K: It is not like that.

DB: So what is it? Is it that the light suddenly turns on, and stays on?

K: No. Because when we say 'stays on' or 'goes off', we are thinking in terms of time.

DB: We have to clear this up, because it is the question everybody will put.

K: The material process is working in darkness, in time, in knowledge, in ignorance and so on. When insight takes place there is the dispelling of that darkness. That is all we are saying. Insight dispels that darkness. And thought, which is the material process, no longer works in darkness. Therefore that light has altered — no, it has ended — ignorance.

DB: So we say that this darkness is really something which is built into the content of thought.

K: The content is darkness.

DB: That's right. Then that light has dispelled that ignorance.

K: That's right. Dispelled the content.

DB: But still we have to be very careful, in case we still have content in the usually accepted sense of the word; you know, all kinds of things.

K: Of course.

DB: So we can't say that the light has dispelled *all* the content.

K: It has dispelled the centre of darkness.

DB: Yes, the source, the creator of darkness.

K: The self. Right? It has dispelled the centre of darkness which is the self.

DB: We could say that the self, which is part of the content — that part of the content which is the centre of darkness, which creates it and maintains it — is dispelled.

K: Yes, I hold to that.

DB: We see now that this means a physical change in the brain cells. That centre, that content which is the centre, is a certain set, form, disposition of all the brain calls, and it in some way alters.

K: Obviously! You see, this has enormous significance, in our relationship with our society, in everything. Now the next question is, how does this flash come about? Let's begin the other way round. How does love come about? How does peace come about? Peace is causeless, violence has cause. How does that causeless thing come about when my whole life ·is causation? There is no 'how' — right? The 'how' implies a cause, so there is no 'how'.

Q: Are you saying that since it is without cause, it is something that just exists . . . ?

K: No, I don't say that it exists. That is a dangerous statement.

Q: It has to exist at some point.

K: No. The moment you say it exists, it is not.

DB: You see, the danger is that it is part of the content.

K: The question you put was about a mutation in the brain calls. That question has been put after a series of discussions. And we have come to a point when we say that the flash, that light, has no cause; that the light operates on that which has cause, which is the darkness. That darkness exists as long as the self is there, it is the originator of that darkness, but light dispels the very centre of darkness. That's all. We have come to that point. And therefore there is a mutation. Then I say that the question of how do I get this flash of insight, how does it happen, is a wrong question. There is no 'how'.

Q: There is no 'how', but there is darkness and there is light.

K: Just see first there is no 'how'. If you show me how, you are back into the darkness. Right?

DB: Yes.

K: It is a tremendous thing to understand that. I am asking something else, which is, why is it that we have no insight at all? Why is it that this insight doesn't start from our childhood?

DB: Well, the way life is lived . . .

K: No, I want to find out. Is it because of our education? Our society? I don't believe it is all that. You follow?

DB: What do you say then?

K: Is it some other factor? I am groping after this. Why don't we have it? It seems so natural.

DB: At first, one would say something is interfering with it.

K: But it seems so natural. For 'X', it is quite natural. Why isn't it natural for everyone? Why isn't it possible? If we talk about blockages, education, etc., which are all in the realm of causation, then to remove the blockages implies another cause. So we keep on rolling in that direction. There is something unnatural about all this.

Q: If you would say that there are blocks . . .

K: I don't want to use that; it is the language of the darkness.

Q: Then you could say that the blocks prevent the insight from acting.

K: Of course. But I want to move away from these blockages.

DB: Not exactly blockages, but we used the words 'centre of darkness', which we say is maintaining darkness.

K: Why isn't it natural for everybody to have this insight?

DB: That is the question.

K: Why is love not natural to everybody? Am I putting the question clearly?

DB: I think, to make it more clear, some people might feel that it is natural to everybody, but being treated in a certain way they gradually get caught in hate.

K: I don't believe that.

DB: Then you would have to suppose that the young child meeting hate would not respond with hate.

K: Yes, that's right.

DB: Most people would say that it is natural for the young child meeting hate to respond with hate.

K: Yes, this morning I heard that. Then I asked myself why? Now just a minute. 'X' has been put under all these circumstances, which could have produced blockages, but 'X' wasn't touched by them. So why is it not possible for everybody?

DB: We should make it clear why we say it would be natural not to respond to hate with hate.

K: All right. Limit it to that.

DB: Even when one hasn't thought about it. You know, the child is not able to think about all this. Some people would say it is instinct, the animal instinct . . .

K: . . . which is to hate . . .

DB: . . . well, to fight back.

K: To fight back.

DB: The animal will respond with love, if you treat him with love, but if you treat the animal with hate he is going to fight back.

K: Of course.

DB: He will become vicious.

K: Yes.

DB: Now some people would say that the human being in the beginning is like that animal, and later he can understand.

K: Of course. That is, the human being's origins were with the animal, and the animal, the ape or the wolf . . .

DB: . . . the wolf will respond with love too.

K: And we are saying, why . . .

DB: Look, almost everybody feels that what I said is true, that when we are very young children, we are like the animal. Now you are asking, why don't all young children immediately fail to respond to hate with hate?

K: That means, is it the fault of the parents?

DB: What you are implying is that it is not entirely that. There must be something deeper.

K: Yes, I think there is something quite different. I want to capture that.

DB: This is something that would be important.

K: How do we find out? Let's have an insight! I feel that there is something totally different. We are attacking it from a causational point of view. Would it be right to say that the beginning of man is not animal?

DB: Well, that is not clear. The present theory of evolution is that there have been apes, developing; you can follow the line where they become more and more like human beings. Now when you say that the beginning of man is not animal, it is not clear.

K: If the beginning of man is the animal, therefore that instinct is natural and then it is highly cultivated.

DB: Yes, that instinct is cause and effect.

K: Cause and effect, and it becomes natural. But someone comes along and asks, 'Is it?'

DB: Let's try to get this clear.

K: I mean, scientists and historians have said that man began from the ape, and that, as all animals respond to love and to hate, we as human beings respond instantly to hate by hate.

DB: And vice versa, to love by love.

K: At the beginning there were a few people who never responded to hate, because they had love. Those people implanted this thing in the human mind. Right? That where love is, hate is not. And that has also been part of our inheritance. Why have we cultivated the response of hate to hate? Why haven't we cultivated the other? Or is the other — love — something that cannot be cultivated?

DB: It is not causal. Cultivation depends on a cause.

K: On thought. So why have we lost the other? We have cultivated very carefully, by thought, the concept of meeting hate by hate, violence by violence, and so on. Why haven't we moved along with the other line? With love, that is causeless? You follow my question?

DB: Yes.

K: Is this a futile question?

DB: One doesn't see any way of proceeding.

K: I am not trying to proceed.

DB: We have to understand what made people respond to hate with hate . . .

K: . . . To 'X', the other seems so natural. So if that is so natural to him, why isn't it natural to everyone else? It *must* be natural to others!
    You know this ancient idea, which is probably in existence in the Jewish and in the Indian religions, and so on, that the manifestation of the highest takes place, occasionally. That seems too easy an explanation. Has mankind moved in the wrong direction? Have we taken a wrong turn?

DB: Yes, we have discussed this before, that there has been a wrong turning.

K: To respond to hate by hate, violence by violence, etc.

DB: And to give supreme value to knowledge.

Q: Wouldn't another factor also be the attempt to cultivate the idea of love? The purpose of the religions has been to produce love, and better human beings.

K: Don't go into all that. Love has no cause, it is not cultivatable. Full stop.

Q: Yes, but the mind doesn't see that.

K: But we have explained all that. I want to find out why, if it is natural to 'X', it isn't natural to others. I think this is a valid question.

DB: Another point is to say that you could see that the response of hate to hate makes no sense anyway. So why do we go on with it? Because many believe in that moment that they are protecting themselves with hate, but it is no protection.

K: But to go back to that question: I think it is valid. 'X' is without cause, 'Y' is caught in cause. Why? You understand? Is it the privilege of the few? The elite? No, no. Let's look at it another way. The mind of humanity has been responding to hate with hate, violence by violence, and knowledge by knowledge. But 'X' is part of humanity, and he does not respond to hate by hate, like 'Y' and 'Z'! They are part of 'X's' consciousness, part of all that.

DB: Why is there this difference?

K: That is what I am asking. One is natural, the other is unnatural. Why? Why the difference? Who is asking this question? The people, 'Y' and 'Z', who respond to hate by hate, are they asking the question? Or is 'X' asking the question?

Q: It would seem that 'X' is asking this question.

DB: Yes, but you see we were also just saying that they are not different. We say they *are* different, but also that they are *not* different.

K: Of course. They are not different.

DB: There is one mind.

K: That's it, one mind.

DB: Yes, and how does it come that another part of this one mind says no?

K: That's the whole thing. How does it come about that one part of the mind says we are different from another? Of course, there are all kinds of explanations, and I am left with the fact that 'A' 'B' and 'C' are different from 'X' 'Y' and 'Z'. And those are facts — right?

Q: They appear to be different.

K: Oh, no.

Q: They are actually different.

K: Absolutely; not just apparently.

DB: I think the question we want to come back to is, why do the people who cultivate hate say that they are different from those who don't?

K: Do they say that?

DB: I think they do, in so far as they would admit that if there was anybody who didn't cultivate hate, they must be different.

K: Yes, that is clear — light and darkness, and so on. But I want to find out if we are moving in the right direction. That is, 'X' has given me that gift, and I have not carried that gift. You follow what I mean? I have cultivated one response, but not carried this. Why? If a father has responded to hate by hate, why has the son not responded in the same way?

DB: I think it is a question of insight.

K: Which means that the son had insight right from the beginning. You follow what I am saying? Right from childhood, which means what?

DB: What?

K: I don't want to enter into this dangerous field yet!

DB: What is it? Perhaps you want to leave that.

K: There is some factor that is missing. I want to capture it. You see, if that is an exception, then it is silly.

DB: All right. Then we agree that the thing is dormant in all human beings; is that what you want to say?

K: I am not quite sure that is what I want to say.

DB: But I meant that the factor is there in all mankind.

K: That is a dangerous statement too.

DB: That is what you were saying.

K: I know, but I am questioning. When I am quite sure, I will tell you.

DB: All right. We tried this, and we can say it seems promising but it is a bit dangerous. This possibility is there in all mankind, and in so far as some people have seen it.

K: Which means God is in you?

DB: No, it is just that the possibility of insight is there.

K: Yes, partly. I am questioning all this. The father responds to hate by hate; the son doesn't.

DB: That happens from time to time.

K: No, consistently from the beginning — why?

DB: It must depend on insight, which shows the futility of hate.

K: Why did that man have it?

DB: Yes, why?

K: And why if this seems so terribly natural to him, is it not natural to everybody? As water is natural to everybody.

DB: Well, why isn't insight present for everybody from the beginning?

K: Yes, that is what I am asking.

DB: So strongly that even maltreatment cannot affect it.

K: Nothing can affect it, that is my point. Maltreatment, beating, being put into all kinds of dreadful situations hasn't affected it. Why? We are coming to something.

15 APRIL 1980, OJAI, CALIFORNIA

SEVEN

Death Has Very Little Meaning

———————————

KRISHNAMURTI: Are we saying that human beings are still behaving with the animal instincts?

DAVID BOHM: Yes, and that the animal instincts, it seems, may be overpowering in their intensity and speed, and especially with young children. It may be that it is only natural for them to respond with the animal instinct.

K: So that means, after a million years, that we are still instinctively behaving like our ancestors?

DB: In some ways. Probably our behaviour is also complicated by thought; the animal instinct has now become entangled with thought, and it is getting in some ways worse.

K: Far worse.

DB: Because all these instincts of hatred now become directed and sustained by thought, so that they are more subtle and dangerous.

K: And during all these many centuries we haven't found a way, a method, a system — something that will move us away from that track. Is that it?

DB: Yes. One of the difficulties, surely, is that when people begin to be angry with each other, their anger builds up and they can't seem to do anything about it. They may try to control it, but that doesn't work.

K: As we were saying, someone — 'X' — behaves naturally in a way that is not a response to the animal instinct. What place has this kind of insight in human society? None at all?

DB: In society as it is, it cannot be accommodated, because society is organized under the assumption that pain and pleasure are going to rule. You could say that friendliness is a kind of animal instinct too, for people become friendly for instinctive reasons. And perhaps they become enemies for similar reasons.

So I think that some people would say that we should be rational rather than instinctive. There was a period during the 18th century, the Age of Reason, when they said man could be rational, could choose to be rational, in order to bring about harmony everywhere.

K: But he hasn't done so!

DB: No, things got worse, leading to the French Revolution, to the Terror and so on. But, after that, people didn't have so much faith in reason as a way of getting anywhere, or coming out of conflict.

K: So where does that lead us? We were talking really about insight that actually changes the nature of the brain itself.

DB: Yes, by dispelling the darkness in the brain, insight allows the brain to function in a new way.

K: Thought has been operating in darkness, creating its own darkness and functioning in that. And insight is, as we said, like a flash which breaks down the darkness. Then when that insight clears the darkness, does man act, or function, rationally?

DB: Yes, man will then function rationally, and with perception, rather than by rules and reason. But there is a freely flowing reason. You see, some people identify reason with certain rules of logic which would be mechanical. But there can be reason as a form of perception of order.

K: So we are saying, are we, that insight is perception?

DB: It is the flash of light which makes perception possible.

K: Right, that's it.

DB: It is even more fundamental than perception.

K: So insight is pure perception, and from that perception there is action, which is then sustained by rationality. Is that it?

DB: Yes.

K: That's right.

DB: And the rationality is perception of order.

K: So, would you say, there is insight, perception and order?

DB: Yes.

K: But that order is not mechanical because it is not based on logic.

DB: There are no rules.

K: No rules; let's put it that way; it's better. This order is not based on rules. This means insight, perception, action, order. Then you come to the question, is insight continuous, or is it by flashes?

DB: We went into that, and felt it was a wrong question, so perhaps we can look at it differently. It is not time binding.

K: Not time binding. Yes, we agreed on that. So now let's get a little further. We said, didn't we, that insight is the elimination of the darkness which is the very centre of the self, the darkness that self creates? Insight dispels that very centre.

DB: Yes. With the darkness, perception is not possible. It's blindness in a way.

K: Right, then what next? I am an ordinary man, with all my animal instincts, pleasure and pain and reward and punishment and so on. I hear you say this, and I see what you are saying has some kind of reason, logic and order.

DB: Yes, it makes sense as far as we can see it.

K: It makes sense. Then how am I to have reason in my life? How am I to bring it about? You understand that these words which are difficult, are all of them time binding. But is that possible?

DB: Yes, without time, you see.

K: Is it possible for man with his narrow mind, to have this insight, so that pattern of life is broken? As we said the other day, we have tried all this, tried every form of self-denial, and yet that insight doesn't come about.

Once in a while there is a partial insight, but that partial insight is not the whole insight, so there is still partial darkness.

DB: Which doesn't dispel the centre of the self. It may dispel some darkness in a certain area, but the source of the darkness, the creator, the sustainer of it, is still there.

K: Still there. Now what shall we do? But this is a wrong question. This leads nowhere.

We have stated the general plan, right? And I have to make the moves, or make no moves at all. I haven't the energy. I haven't the capacity to see it quickly. Because this is immediate, not just something that I practise and eventually get. I haven't the capacity, I haven't the sense of urgency, of immediacy. Everything is against me: my family, my wife, society. *Everything!* And does this mean that I eventually have to become a monk?

DB: No. Becoming a monk is the same as becoming anything else.

K: That's right. Becoming a monk is like becoming a business-man! I see all this, verbally as well as rationally, intellectually, but I can't capture this thing. Is there a different approach to this problem? I am always asking the same question, because I am caught in the same pattern. So, is there a totally different way? A totally different approach to the whole turmoil of life? Is there a different manner of looking at it? Or is the old way the only way?

We have said that as long as the centre is creating darkness, and thought is operating in that darkness, there must be disorder, and society will be as it is now. To move away from that, you must have insight. Insight can only come about when there is a flash, a sudden light, which abolishes not only darkness but the creator of darkness.

DB: Yes.

K: Now I am asking if there is a different approach to this question altogether, although an old response seems so absolute.

DB: Well possibly. When you say it seems absolute, do you want a less absolute approach?

K: I am saying that if that *is* the only way, then we are doomed.

DB: You can't produce this flash at will.

K: No, it can't be produced through will, through sacrifice, through any form of human effort. That is out; we know we have finished with all that. And also we agreed that to some people — to 'X' — this insight seemed so natural and we asked why is it not natural to others?

DB: If we begin with the child, it seems natural to the child to respond with his animal instincts, with great intensity which sweeps him away. Darkness arises because it is so overwhelming.

K: Yes, but why is it different with 'X'?

DB: First of all it seems natural to most people that the animal instincts would take over.

K: Yes, that's right.

DB: And they would say the other fellow, 'X', is unnatural.

K: Yes.

DB: So that is the way mankind has been thinking, saying that if there are indeed any people who are different they must be very unusual and unnatural.

K: That's it. Human beings have been responding to hatred by hatred, and so on. There are those few, perhaps many, who say that is not natural or rational. Why has this division taken place?

DB: If we say that pleasure and pain, fear and hate, are natural, then it is felt that we must battle to control these, otherwise they will destroy us. The best we can hope for is to control them with reason, or through another way.

K: But that doesn't work! Are people like 'X', who function differently, the privileged few, by some miracle, by some strange chance event?

DB: Many people would say that.

K: But it goes against one's grain. I would not accept that.

DB: Well, if that is not the case, then you have to say why there is this difference.

K: That is what I am trying to get at, because 'X' is born of the same parents.

DB: Yes, fundamentally the same, so why does he behave differently?

K: This question has been asked many times, over and over again in different parts of the world. Now why is there this division?

QUESTIONER: Is the division really total? You see, even the man who responds to hatred with hatred, nevertheless sees that it doesn't make sense, is not natural and should be different.

K: It should be different, but he is still battling with ideas. He is trying to get out of it by the exercise of thought which breeds darkness.

Q: I just want to say that the division does not seem to be so entire.

K: Oh, but the division *is* entire, complete.

Q: Well, then, why are people not simply saying, let's continue to live that way, and let's enjoy it to the last moment?

K: Because they can't see anything except their own darkness.

Q: But they want to get out of it.

K: Now wait a minute. Do they want to get out of it? Do they actually realize the state they are in, and deliberately want to get out of it?

Q: They are ambivalent about it. They want to go on getting the fruits of it, but they have a sense that it is wrong, and that it leads to suffering.

DB: Or else they find they can't help it. You see, when the time comes to experience anger or pleasure, they can't get away.

K: They can't help it.

Q: But they want to get out of it, although they are helpless. There are forces which are stronger than their will.

K: So what shall we do? or is this divison false?

DB: That's the point. We had better talk of a difference between these two approaches. This difference is not fundamental.

K:˙ I don't think they have anything in common.

DB: Why? You say the difference is false, although fundamentally people are the same, but a difference has developed between them. Perhaps most people have taken a wrong turning.

K: Yes, let's put it that way.

DB: But the difference is not intrinsic, it is not structural, built in like the difference between a tree and a rock.

K: Agreed. As you say, there is a difference between a rock and a tree, but it is not like that. Let's be simple. There are two responses. They start from the source; one has taken one direction, and the other has taken a different direction. But the source is the same. Why haven't all of them moved in the right direction?

DB: We haven't managed to answer that. I was just saying that if one understands that, then going back to the source, one does not have to take the wrong turn. In a sense we are continually taking this wrong turn, so if we can understand this, then it becomes possible to change. And we are continually starting from the same source, not going back in time to a source.

K: Just a minute, just a minute.

DB: There are two possible ways of taking our statement. One is to say that the source is in time, that far back in the past we started together and took different paths. The other is to say that the source is timeless, and we are continually taking the wrong turn, again and again. Right?

K: Yes, it is constantly the wrong turn. Why?

Q: This means that there is the constant possibility of the right turn.

K: Yes, of course. That's it. If we say there is a source from which we all began, then we are caught in time.

DB: We can't go back.

K: No, that is out. Therefore it is apparent that we are taking the wrong turn all the time.

DB: Constantly.

K: Constantly taking the wrong turn. But why? The one who is living with insight and the other who is not living with insight —

are these constant? The man who is living in darkness can move away at any time to the other. That is the point. At any time.

DB: Then nothing holds him, except constantly taking the wrong turn. You could say the darkness is such that he doesn't see himself taking the wrong turn.

K: Are we pursuing the right direction, putting the right question? Suppose you have that insight, and your darkness, the very centre of darkness, has been dispelled completely. And I, a serious, fairly intelligent human being, listen to you. And whatever you have said seems reasonable, rational, sane. I question the division. The division is created by the centre which creates darkness. Thought has created it.

DB: Well, in darkness, thought creates the division.

K: From the darkness a shadow is thrown; it makes a division.

DB: If we have that insight, we say there is no division.

K: Yes. And man won't accept that, because in his darkness there is nothing but division. So we, living in darkness, have created the division. We have created it in our thoughts . . .

DB: We are constantly creating it.

K: Yes, always wanting to live constantly in a state in which there is no division. That movement, however, is still the movement of darkness. Right?

DB: Yes.

K: How am I to dispel this continuous, constant darkness? That is the only question, because, as long as that exists, I create this constant division. You see, this is going round in circles. I can only dispel the darkness through insight, and I cannot have that insight by any effort of will, so I am left with nothing. So what is my problem? My problem is to perceive the darkness, to perceive the thought that is creating darkness, and to see that the self is the source of this darkness. Why can't I see that? Why can't I see it even logically?

DB: Well, it's clear logically.

K: Yes, but somehow it doesn't seem to operate. So what shall I do? I realize for the first time that the self is creating the darkness which is constantly breeding division. I see that very clearly.

DB: And the division produces the darkness anyway.

K: Vice versa, back and forth. And from all that, everything begins. I see that very clearly. What shall I do? So I don't admit division.

Q: Krishnaji, aren't we introducing division again, nevertheless, when we say there is the man who needs insight?

K: But man has insight. 'X' has insight, and he has explained very clearly how darkness has vanished. I listen to him, and he says your very darkness is creating the division. Actually, there is no division, no division as light and darkness. So he asks me, can you banish, can you put away this sense of division?

DB: You seem to be bringing back a division by saying that, by saying that I should do it, you see.

K: No, not 'should'.

DB: In a way you are saying that the thought process of the mind seems spontaneously to produce division. You say, try to put it aside, and at the same time it is trying to make division.

K: I understand. But can my mind put away division? Or is that a wrong question?

Q: Can it put away division as long as it is divided?

K: No, it can't. So what am I to do?
    Listen. 'X' says something so extraordinarily true, of such immense significance and beauty that my whole being says 'Capture it'. That is not a division.
    I recognize that I am the creator of division, because I am living in darkness, and so out of that darkness I create. But I have listened to 'X', who says there is no division. And I recognize that is an extraordinary statement. So the very saying of that to one who has lived in constant division has an immediate effect. Right?

DB: I think that one has to, as you say, put away the division . . .

K: I will leave that; I won't put it away. That statement that there is no division — I want to get at that a little bit. I am getting somewhere with it.

'X' s' statement from this insight, that there is no division has a tremendous effect on me. I have lived constantly in division, and he comes along and says there is no division. What effect has it on me?

DB: Then you say there is no division. That makes sense. But on the other hand it seems that the division exists.

K: I recognize the division, but the statement that there is no division has this immense impact on me. That seems natural, doesn't it? When I see something that is immovable, it must have some effect on me. I respond to it with a tremendous shock.

DB: You see, if you were talking about something which was in front of us, and you said, 'No, it is not that way', then that would, of course, change your whole way of seeing it. Now you say this division is not that way. We try to look and see if that is so — right?

K: I don't even say, 'Is that so?' 'X' has very carefully explained the whole business, and he says at the end of it that there is no division. And I am sensitive, watching very carefully, and realizing that I am constantly living in division. When 'X' makes that statement it has broken the pattern.

I don't know if you follow what I am trying to explain? It has broken the pattern, because he has said something which is so fundamentally true. There is no God and man. Right, Sir, I stick to that. I see something — which is, where hatred exists the other is not. But, hating, I want the other. So constant division is born out of darkness. And the darkness is constant. But I have been listening very carefully, and 'X' makes a statement which seems absolutely true. That enters into me, and the act of his statement dispels the darkness. I am not making an effort to get rid of darkness, but 'X' is the light. That's right, I hold to that.

So it comes to something, which is, can I listen with my darkness — in my darkness, which is constant? In that darkness, can I listen to you? Of course I can. I am living in constant division which brings darkness. 'X' comes along and tells me there is no division.

DB: Right. Now why do you say you can listen in the darkness?

K: Oh, yes, I can listen in darkness. If I can't I am doomed.

DB: But that is no argument.

K: Of course that is no argument, but it is so!

DB: Living in darkness is not worth-while. But now we say that it is possible to listen in the darkness.

K: He, 'X', explains to me very, very carefully. I am sensitive, I have been listening to him in my darkness, but that is making me sensitive, alive, watching. That is what I have been doing. We have been doing it together. And he makes a statement that there is absolutely no division. And I know that I am living in division. That very statement has brought the constant movement to an end.

Otherwise, if this doesn't take place I have nothing — you follow? I am *perpetually* living in darkness. But there is a voice in the wilderness, and listening to that voice has an extraordinary effect.

DB: Listening reaches the source of the movement, whereas observation does not.

K: Yes, I have observed, I have listened, I have played all kinds of games all my life. And I now see, that there is only one thing. That there is this constant darkness and I am acting in the darkness; in this wilderness which is darkness; whose centre is the self. I see that *absolutely*, completely; I can't argue against it any more. And 'X' comes along and tells me this. In that wilderness a voice says there is water. You follow? It is not hope. There is immediate action in me.

One must realize, that this constant movement in darkness is my life. You follow what I am saying? Can I, with all the experience, with all the knowledge which I have gathered over a million years, suddenly realize that I am living in total darkness? Because that means I have reached the end of all hope. Right? But my hope is also darkness. The future is out altogether, so I am left with this enormous darkness, and I am there. That means, the realization of that is the ending of becoming. I have reached that point and 'X' tells me this is natural.

You see, all the religions have said this division exists.

DB: But, they say it can be overcome.

K: It is the same pattern repeated. It doesn't matter who said it, but the fact is somebody in this wilderness is saying something, and in that wilderness I have been listening to every voice, and to my own voice, which has created more and more darkness. Yet, this is right. That means doesn't it, that when there is insight there is no division?

DB: Yes.

K: It is not your insight or my insight, it is insight. In that there is no division.

DB: Yes.

K: Which brings us to that ground we spoke of . . .

DB: What about the ground?

K: In that ground there is no darkness as darkness, or light as light. In that ground, there is no division. Nothing is born of will, or time, or thought.

DB: Are you saying that light and darkness are not divided?

K: Right.

DB: Which means to say there is neither.

K: Neither, that's it! There is something else. There is a perception that there is a different movement, which is 'non-dualistic'.

DB: Non-dualistic means what? No division.

K: No division. I won't use 'non-dualistic'. There is no division.

DB: But nevertheless there is movement.

K: Of course.

DB: What does that mean now, without division?

K: I mean by movement, that movement which is not time. That movement doesn't breed division. So I want to go back, lead to the ground. If, in that ground, there is neither darkness nor light, no God or the son of God — there is no division — what takes place? Would you say that the ground is movement?

DB: Well, it could be, yes. Movement is undivided.

K: No. I say there is movement in darkness.

DB: Yes, but we said there is no division of darkness and light, and yet you said there is movement.

K: Yes. Would you say the ground is endless movement?

DB: Yes.

K: What does that mean?

DB: Well, it is difficult to express.

K: Keep on going into it; let's express it. What is movement, apart from movement from here to there, apart from time — is there any other movement?

DB: Yes.

K: There is. The movement from being to becoming, psychologically. There is the movement of distance, there is the movement of time. We say those are all divisions. Is there a movement which in itself has no division? When you have made that statement that there is no division, there is that movement surely?

DB: Well, are you saying that when there is no division that movement is there?

K: Yes, and I said, 'X' says that is the ground.

DB: Right.

K: Would you say it has no end, no beginning?

DB: Yes.

K: Which means again time.

DB: Can one say that movement has no form?

K: No form — all that. I want to go a little further. What I am asking is, we said that when you have stated there is no division, this means no division in movement.

DB: It flows without division, you see.

K: Yes, it is a movement in which there is no division. Do I capture the significance of that? Do I understand the depth of that statement? A movement in which there is no division, which means no time, no distance as we know it. No element of time in it at all. So I am trying to see if that movement is surrounding man?

DB: Yes, enveloping.

K: I want to get at this. I am concerned with mankind, humanity, which is me. 'X' has made several statements, and I have captured a statement which seems so absolutely true – that there is no division. Which means that there is no action which is divisive.

DB: Yes.

K: I see that. And I also ask, is that movement without time, etc? It seems that it is the world, you follow?

DB: The universe.

K: The universe, the cosmos, the whole.

DB: The totality.

K: Totality. Isn't there a statement in the Jewish world, 'Only God can say I am'?

DB: Well, that's the way the language is built. It is not necessary to state it.

K: No, I understand. You follow what I am trying to get at?

DB: Yes, that only this movement *is*.

K: Can the mind be of that movement? Because that is timeless, therefore deathless.

DB: Yes, the movement is without death; in so far as the mind takes part in that, it is the same.

K: You understand what I am saying?

DB: Yes. But what dies when the individual dies?

K: That has no meaning, because once I have understood there is no division . . .

DB: . . . then it is not important.

K: Death has no meaning.

DB: It still has a meaning in some other context.

K: Oh, the ending of the body; that's totally trivial. But you understand? I want to capture the significance of the statement that there is no division, it has broken the spell of my darkness, and I see that there is a movement, and that's all. Which means death has very little meaning.

DB: Yes.

K: You have abolished totally the fear of death.

DB: Yes, I understand that when the mind is partaking in that movement, then the mind *is* that movement.

K: That's all! the mind is that movement.

DB: Would you say that matter is also that movement?

K: Yes, I would say everything is. In my darkness I have listened to 'X'. That's most important. And his clarity has broken my spell. When he said there is no division, he abolished the division between life and death. I don't know if you see this?

DB: Yes.

K: One can never say then, 'I am immortal'. It is so childish.

DB: Yes, that's the division.

K: Or, 'I am seeking immortality'. Or, 'I am becoming'. We have wiped away the whole sense of moving in darkness.

Q: What then would be the significance of the world? Is there a significance to it?

K: The world?

Q: With man.

DB: Society, do you mean?

Q: Yes, it seems that when you make that statement, there is no division, and life is death — what then is the significance of man with all his struggle. . . ?

K: Man in darkness. What importance has that? It is like struggling in a locked room. That is the whole point.

DB: Significance can only rise when the darkness is dispelled.

K: Of course.

Q: The only significance is the dispelling of the darkness.

K: Oh, no, no!

DB: Aren't we going to say that something more can be done besides dispelling the darkness?

K: I have listened very carefully to everything that you, who have insight, say. What you have done is to dispel the centre. In darkness I could invent many things of significance; that there is light, there is God, there is beauty, there is this and that. But it is still in the area of darkness. Caught in a room full of darkness, I can invent a lot of pictures, but I want to get something else. Is the mind the one who has this insight — who therefore dispels darkness and has understanding of the ground which is movement without time — is that mind itself the movement?

DB: Yes, but it isn't the totality. The mind is the movement, but we are saying movement is matter, movement is mind. And we were saying that the ground may be beyond the universal mind. You said earlier that the movement, that the ground, is more than the universal mind, more than the emptiness.

K: We said that; much more.

DB: Much more. But we have to get this clear. We say that the mind is this movement.

K: Yes, mind is the movement.

DB: We are not saying that this movement is only mind?

K: No, no, no.

DB: That is the point I was trying to get correct.

K: Mind is the movement — mind, in the sense, 'the ground'.

DB: But you said that the ground goes beyond the mind.

K: Now just a minute: what do you mean by 'beyond the mind'?

DB: Just going back to what we were discussing a few days ago: we said we have the emptiness, the universal mind, and then the ground is beyond that.

K: Would you say beyond that is this movement?

DB: Yes. The mind emerges from the movement as a ground, and falls back to the ground; that is what we are saying.

K: Yes, that's right. Mind emerges from the movement.

DB: And it dies back into the movement.

K: That's right. It has its being in the movement.

DB: Yes, and matter also.

K: Quite. So, what I want to get at is, I am a human being faced with this ending and beginning. And 'X' abolishes that.

DB: Yes, it is not fundamental.

K: It is not fundamental. One of the greatest fears of life, which is death, has been removed.

DB: Yes.

K: You see what it does to a human being when there is no death? It means the mind doesn't age — the ordinary mind I am talking about. I don't know if I am conveying this.

DB: Let's go slowly. You say the mind does not age, but what if the brain cells age?

K: I question it.

DB: But how can we know that?

K: Because there is no conflict, because there is no strain, there is no becoming, no movement.

DB: This is something that it is hard to communicate with certainty about.

K: Of course. You can't prove any of this.

DB: But the other, what we have said so far . . .

K: . . . can be reasoned.

DB: It is reason, and also you can feel it. But now you are stating something about the brain cells that I have no feeling for. It might be so; it could be so.

K: I think it *is* so. I won't discuss it. When a mind has lived in the darkness and is in constant movement there is the wearing out, the decay of the cells.

DB: We could say that this conflict will cause cells to decay. But somebody might argue that perhaps even without conflict they could decay at a slower rate. Let's say if you were to live hundreds of years, for example, in time the cells would decay no matter what you did.

K: Go into this slowly.

DB: I can readily accept that the rate of decay of the cells could be cut down when we get rid of conflict.

K: Decay can be slowed down.

DB: Perhaps a great deal.

K: A great deal. Ninety per cent.

DB: That we could understand. But if you say a hundred per cent, then it is hard to understand.

K: Ninety per cent. Wait a minute. It can be very, very greatly slowed down. And that means what? What happens to a mind that has no conflict? What is that mind, what is the quality of that mind which has no problem? You see, suppose such a mind lives in pure unpolluted air, having the right kind of food and so on, why can't it live two hundred years?

DB: Well it is possible; some people have lived for a hundred and fifty years, living in very pure air, and eating good food.

K: But you see, if those very people who have lived a hundred and fifty years, had no conflict, they might live very much longer.

DB: They might. There was a case I was reading of a man in England who lived to be a hundred and fifty. And the doctors became interested in him. They wined and dined him, and then he died in a few days!

K: Poor devil!

Q: Krishnaji, you generally say that anything that lives in time, also dies in time.

K: Yes, but the brain, which has had insight, has changed the cells.

Q: Are you implying that even the organic brain does not live in time any more?

K: No, don't bring in time yet. We are saying that insight brings about a change in the brain cells. Which means that the brain cells are no longer thinking in terms of time.

Q: Psychological time?

K: Of, course, that is understood.

DB: If they are not so disturbed, they will remain in order and perhaps they will break down more slowly. We might increase the age limit from one hundred and fifty to two hundred years, provided one also had healthy living at all levels.

K: Yes, but all that sounds so very trivial.

DB: Yes, it doesn't seem to make much difference, although it is an interesting idea.

K: What if I live another hundred years? We are trying to find out what effect this extraordinary movement has on the brain.

DB: Yes. If we say the brain is in some way directly enveloped in this movement; that would bring it to order. But there is a real direct flow, physically.

K: Not only physically.

DB: But also mentally.

K: Yes, both. It must have an extraordinary effect on the brain.

Q: You talked earlier about energy. Not the everyday energy . . .

K: We said that that movement is total energy. Now this insight has captured, seen, that extraordinary movement, and it is part of that energy. I want to come much closer to earth; I have lived with the fear of death, fear of not becoming, and so on. Suddenly I see there is no division, and I understand the whole thing. So what has happened to my brain — you follow?

Let's *see* something. See this whole thing, not verbally, but as a tremendous reality, as truth. With all your heart, mind, you see this thing. That very perception must affect your brain.

DB: Yes. It brings order.

K: Not only order in life but in the brain.

DB: People can prove that if you are under stress the brain cells start to break down. And if you have order in the brain cells, then it is quite different.

K: I have a feeling, Sir — don't laugh at it; it may be false, it may be true — I feel that the brain never loses the quality of that movement.

DB: Once it has it.

K: Of course. I am talking of the person who has been through all this.

DB: So probably the brain never loses that quality.

K: Therefore it is no longer involved in time.

DB: It would no longer be dominated by time. The brain, from what we were saying, is not evolving in any sense, it is just a confusion. You can't say that man's brain has evolved during the last ten thousand years. You see science, knowledge, has evolved, but people felt the same about life several thousand years ago as they do now.

K: I want to find out: in that silent emptiness that we went through, is the brain absolutely still? In the sense, no movement.

DB: Not absolutely. You see, the blood is going in the brain.

K: We are not talking of that.

DB: What kind of movement are we discussing?

K: I am talking of the movement of thought, the movement of *any* reaction.

DB: Yes. There is no movement in which the brain moves independently. You were saying that there is the movement of the whole, but the brain does not go off on its own, as thought.

K: You see, you have abolished death, which is a tremendously significant thing. And so I say, what is the brain, the mind, when there is no death. You follow? It has undergone a surgical operation.

DB: We said the brain normally has the notion of death continually there in the background, and that notion is constantly disturbing the brain, because the brain foresees death, and it is trying to stop it.

K: To stop the ending of itself, and so on.

DB: It foresees all that, and thinks it must stop it, but it can't.

K: It can't.

DB: And therefore it has a problem.

K: A constant struggle with it. So all that has come to an end. What an extraordinary thing has taken place! How does it affect my daily life, because I have to live on this earth? My daily life is aggression, this everlasting becoming, striving for success — all that has gone. We will pursue this but we have understood a great deal today.

DB: In bringing in the question of daily life you might bring in the question of compassion.

K: Of course. Is that movement compassion?

DB: It would be beyond.

K: That's it. That's why one must be awfully careful.

DB: Then again, compassion might emerge out of it.

17 APRIL 1980, OJAI, CALIFORNIA

EIGHT

Can Insight be Awakened in Another?

———————————

KRISHNAMURTI: We were discussing what it is for the brain to have no movement. When a human being has been pursuing the path of becoming, and has gone through all that, and this sense of emptiness, silence and energy, he has abandoned almost every-thing and come to the point, the ground. So how does this insight affect his daily life? What is his relationship to society? What is his action with regard to war, and the whole world — a world that is really living and struggling in darkness? What is his action? I would say, as we agreed the other day, that it is non-movement.

DAVID BOHM: Yes, we said before that the ground was move-ment without division.

K: Without division. Yes, quite.

DB: In some sense it seems inconsistent to say non-movement, while you say the ground is movement.

K: Yes, the ground is movement. Would you say an average, educated, sophisticated man, with all his unpleasant activities, is constantly in movement?

DB: Well, a certain kind of movement.

K: A movement in time.

DB: Yes.

K: A movement in becoming. But we are discussing the man who has trodden that path (if I may use that word), and come to that point. From there, what is his action? We said, for the moment, non-action, non-movement. What does that mean?

DB: It means, as you said, not taking part in this process of becoming.

K: Of course, that is obvious. If he doesn't take part in this process, what part does he play? Is it one of complete non-action?

DB: It is not clear why you should call it non-action. We might think that it was action of another kind, which is not part of the process of becoming.

K: It is not becoming.

DB: But it may still be action.

K: He still has to live in the world.

DB: In one sense, whatever you do is action, but his action is not directed towards the illusory process, it is not involved in it, but would be directed towards what underlies this illusory process. It would be directed perhaps towards considering the wrong turning which is continually coming out of the ground. Right?

K: Yes, yes. You see, various religions have described a man who has been saved, who is illuminated, who has achieved something or other. They have described very clearly, especially in Hindu religious books, how he walks, how he looks, how he talks, the whole state of his being. I think that is merely a poetic description which . . .

DB: You think it is imagination?

K: I think a great deal of it is imagination. I have discussed this point with some, and it is not like that, not imagination. Somebody who describes it, knows exactly what it is.

DB: Well, how should he know? It is not clear.

K: So what is a man of that kind? How does he live in this world? This is a very interesting question, if you go into it deeply. There is a state of non-movement. That is, the non-movement which we have gone into.

DB: You see, it is not clear exactly what you mean by non-movement.

K: One becomes poetic but I am trying to avoid that! Although it would be right, even poetically: it is like a single tree in a field. There is no other tree, but that tree, whatever the name of that tree is, it is there.

DB: But why do you say, 'non-movement'?

K: It is non-moving.

DB: The tree stands of course.

K: A tree is a living, moving thing. I don't mean that.

DB: The tree in a sense is moving, but in relation to the field it stands. That is the picture we get.

K: You see, someone comes to you, because you have gone from the beginning to the end. And now you are at the end with a totally different kind of movement, which is timeless, and all that. You are in that. I come to you and ask, 'What is that state of mind? What is the state of your mind, that has walked on that path and ended something, that has totally moved out of darkness?'

DB: If you say it is non-movement, are you implying that it is constant?

K: It must be . . . But what do you mean by constant? Continuous?

DB: No, no.

K: Do you mean that it is . . . ?

QUESTIONER: . . . static?

K: Oh, no!

DB: To stand firm, to stand together as a whole. That is really its literal meaning.

K: Is that it?

DB: That is the picture you have got of the tree as well. That is the picture which the tree in the field suggests.

K: Yes, I know. That is too romantic and poetic, and it becomes rather deceptive. It is a nice image, but let's move from it. What is that mind? The quality of that mind that has started from the beginning, and pursued the becoming, and gone through all that centre of darkness which has been wiped away? That mind must be entirely different. Now what does such a mind do, or not do, in the world which is in darkness?

DB: Surely the mind does not do a thing; it does not enter into the movement of that world.

K: Agreed.

DB: And in a sense we say that it is constant — not fixed, but it does not move.

K: Is it static?

DB: No, it's not static. It is constant — which in a sense is also movement. There is a constancy which is not merely static, which is also, at the same time, movement.

K: We said *that* movement was not the becoming movement.

DB: Yes, but the ground movement which is completely free.

K: What has happened to that mind? Let's go into it a little bit. It has no anxiety and no fear. You see the words 'compassion' and 'love' are beyond that. Right?

DB: But they may emerge out of this ground.

K: The mind being nothing, not a *thing*, and therefore empty of knowledge, would it always be acting in the light of insight?

DB: It would be pervaded, if not always, by the quality of insight.

K: Yes, that is what I mean.

DB: Well 'always' brings in time, you see.

K: Remove the word.

DB: I would use 'constantly'.

K: Yes, constantly; let's use the word 'constant'.

DB: It is a bit better, but not good enough.

K: Yes. Let's use that word. It is acting constantly in that light, in that flash of insight. I think that is right. So what does that mean in one's daily life? How does one earn a livelihood?

DB: That, surely, would be another point. You would have to find a way to stay alive.

K: Stay alive. So that is why I am saying this: as civilization grows, begging is not allowed.

DB: Is criminal. You have to find some way to stay alive.

K: So what will he do? He has no profession, no special skill, no coin with which he can buy.

DB: Well, wouldn't it be possible for this mind to earn enough to get what is needed to stay alive?

K: How?

Q: Why has he no skill to earn a livelihood?

K: Why should he have skill? Why must one have skill to earn a livelihood? You say that, and another man says, 'Why should I have skill of any kind?' I am just discussing, enquiring into this.

DB: Suppose you had to take care of yourself, you would need a certain skill. If you were by yourself in a cave, you know . . .

K: Ah, I don't want a cave!

DB: I know. But, whoever it is, he has to live somewhere; *he* needs some skill to find the food which he needs. You see, if everybody were to say no skill is needed then the human race would perish.

K: I am not sure.

DB: Well, what would happen then?

K: That is what I am coming to. Skill implies, as we said, knowledge; from knowledge, comes experience, and gradually one develops a skill. And that skill gives one an opportunity to earn a livelihood, either meagre or rich. But this man says, there may be a different way of living and earning. We are used to a pattern, and he says, 'Look, that may be totally wrong'.

DB: It depends what you mean by skill. For example, suppose he has to drive a car, surely that takes some skill?

K: Yes.

DB: Is he going to do without that?

K: I had better go carefully into the word 'skill'.

DB: Yes. I mean skill could have a bad meaning — like being very clever at getting money.

K: So this man is not avaricious, he is not money-minded, he is not storing up for the future, he hasn't any insurance. But he has to live. When we use the word 'skill' to mean driving a car . . .

DB: ... or being a carpenter ... If all those skills were to vanish, life would be impossible.

K: The whole thing would collapse.

DB: Yes.

K: I am not sure. Do we mean that kind of skill must be denied?

DB: It couldn't mean that.

K: No. That would be too silly.

DB: But then people become very skilful at getting other people to give them money, you see!

Q: Is it that now we have made a division between living and skill, skill and working, living and earning a livelihood?

K: That's it! I need to have food, I need to have clothes, and shelter.

Q: But is the division necessary? As society is built now, we have a division between living and working.

K: We have been through all that. We are talking of a man who has been through all this, and has come back to the world, and says, 'Here I am'. What is his relationship to society, and what is he to do? Has he any relationship to society?

DB: Well, not in a deep or fundamental sense, although there is a superficial relationship that he has to have.

K: All right. A superficial contact with the world.

DB: He has to obey the laws, he has to follow the traffic signals.

K: Quite. But I want to find out, what is he to do? Write? Talk? That means skill.

DB: Surely that kind of skill need not be harmful?

K: I am just asking.

DB: Like the other skills; like carpentry.

K: Yes. That kind of skill. But what is he to do? I think if we could find out the quality of a mind that has been through all that from the beginning to the end, all that we have talked of in our recent discussions; that man's mind is entirely different, yet he is in the world. How does he look upon it? You have reached and come back — these are approximate terms — and I am an ordinary man, living in this world. So what is your relationship to me? Obviously none, because I am living in a world of darkness and you are not. So your relationship can only exist when I come out of it — when darkness ends.

DB: Yes.

K: Then there is only that; there is not a relationship. But now there is division between you and me. And I look at you with my eyes, which are accustomed to darkness and to division. But you are not. And yet you have to have some contact with me. You have to have, however superficial, however slight, a certain relationship with me. Is that relationship compassion, and not something translated by me as compassion? From my darkness I cannot judge what compassion is. Right?

DB: Yes. That follows from that.

K: I don't know what your love is, what your compassion is because my only love and compassion has been this. And so, what do I do with you?

DB: Who are we talking about now? It is not clear to me whom we are discussing!

K: You or 'X', have been through all that, and come back.

DB: Then why hasn't 'Y' done so?

K: 'Y' has not. 'Y' asks, 'Who are you? You seem so different. Your way of looking at life is different.' And what will 'Y' do with 'X'? That is the question. Not what will 'X' do to 'Y'. I don't know if I am making it clear.

DB: Yes, I understand. What will 'Y' do with 'X'?

K: Our question until now has been what will 'X' do with 'Y', but I think we were putting the wrong question. What will 'Y' do with 'X'? I think what would happen generally is that 'Y' would worship, kill or neglect him. Right?

DB: Yes.

K: If 'Y' worships 'X' then everything is very simple. He has the goodies of the world. But that doesn't answer my question. My question is not only what will 'Y' do to 'X', but what will 'X' do with 'Y'? 'X's' demand is, 'Look, walk out of this darkness; there is no answer in the darkness, so walk out.' It doesn't matter, whatever phrase we use — walk out, dispel it, get rid of it, etc. And 'Y' then says, 'Help me, show me the way', and is back again in darkness — you follow? So what will 'Y' do to 'X'?

DB: I can't see that 'Y' can do very much, except what you mentioned — to worship, or to do something else.

K: To kill or neglect 'X'.

DB: But if compassion works in 'X' . . .

K: Yes, 'X' is that. He won't even call it compassion.

DB: No, but we call it that. Then 'X' will work to find a way to penetrate the darkness.

K: Wait! So 'X's job is to work on darkness?

DB: To discover how to penetrate darkness.

K: In that way he is earning a living.

DB: Well, possibly.

K: No. I am talking seriously.

DB: It depends on whether people are willing to pay him for it.

K: No joking. Seriously.

DB: It is possible.

K: Probably 'X' is the teacher. 'X' is out of society. 'X' is unrelated to this field of darkness and saying to the people who are caught in it, 'Come out'. What's wrong with that?

DB: Nothing is wrong with that.

K: That is his means of livelihood.

DB: It's perfectly all right as long as it works. Of course, if there were a lot of people like 'X', there would have to be some limit.

K: No, Sir. What would happen if there were lots of people like 'X'?

DB: That is an interesting question. I think there would be something revolutionary.

K: That's just it.

DB: The whole thing would change.

K: Yes. If there were lots of people like that, they would not be divided. That is the whole point, right?

DB: I think that even if ten or fifteen people were undivided they would exert a force that has never been seen in our history.

K: Tremendous! That's right.

DB: Because I don't think it has ever happened, that ten people have been undivided.

K: That is 'X's' job in life. He says that is the only thing. A group of those ten 'X's' will bring a totally different kind of revolution. Will society stand for that?

DB: They will have this extreme intelligence, and so they will find a way to do it, you see.

K: Of course.

DB: Society will stand for it, because the 'X's' will be intelligent enough not to provoke society, and society will not react before it is too late.

K: Quite right. You are saying something which is actually happening. Would you say then that the function of many 'X's' is to awaken human beings to that intelligence which will dispel the darkness? And that this is 'X's' means of livelihood?

DB: Yes.

K: Then there are those people who in darkness cultivate this and exploit people, but there are 'X's' who don't exploit. All right. That *seems* very simple, but I don't think it *is* all that simple.

DB: Right.

K: Is that the only function of 'X'?

DB: Well it is really a difficult function.

K: But I want to find out something much deeper than mere function.

DB: Yes, function is not enough.

K: That's it. Apart from function, what is he to do? 'X' says to 'Y', 'Listen'; And 'Y' takes time, and gradually, perhaps, at some time he will wake up and move away. And is that all 'X' is going to do in life?

DB: That can only be an outcome of something deeper.

K: The deeper is all that; the ground.

DB: Yes, the ground.

K: But is that all he is to do in this world? Just to teach people to move out of darkness?

DB: Well, that seems to be the prime task at the moment, in the sense that, if this doesn't happen, the whole society will sooner or later collapse. We could ask whether he needs to be in some sense more deeply creative.

K: What is that?

DB: Well, it is not clear.

K: Suppose 'X' is you, and you have an enormous field in which to operate, not merely teaching me but having this extraordinary movement which is not of time. That is, you have this abounding energy, and you have produced all that to teach me to come out of darkness.

DB: That can only be a part of it.

K: So what does the rest do, you follow? I don't know if I am conveying this.

DB: Well, this is what I tried to suggest by talking of some creative action, beyond this, taking place.

K: Yes, beyond this. You may write, you may preach, you may heal, you may do this and that, but all those activities are rather trivial. But you have something else. Have I reduced you, 'X', to my pettiness? You can't be so reduced. My pettiness says, 'You must do something. You must preach, write, heal, do something to help me to move.' Right? You comply to the very smallest degree, but you have something much more than that, something immense. You understand my question?

DB: Yes. So what happens?

K: How is that immensity operating on 'Y'?

DB: Are you saying that there is some more direct action?

K: Either there is more direct action, or 'X' is doing something totally different to affect the consciousness of man.

DB: What could this be?

K: Because 'X' is not 'satisfied' with merely preaching and talking. That immensity which he is must have an effect, must do something.

DB: Are you saying 'must' in the sense of the feeling of needing to do it, or are you saying 'must' in the sense of necessity?

K: It must.

DB: It must necessarily do so. But how will it affect mankind? You see, when you say this, it would suggest to people that there is some sort of extra-sensory effect that spreads.

K: That is what I am trying to capture.

DB: Yes.

K: That is what I am trying to convey.

DB: Not merely through the words, through the activities or gestures.

K: Let's leave the activity alone. That is simple. It is not just that, because that immensity must . . .

DB: . . . Necessarily act? There is a more direct action?

K: No, no. All right. That immensity necessarily has other activities.

DB: Other activities at other levels?

K: Yes, other activities. This has been translated in the Hindu teachings as various degrees of consciousness.

DB: There are different levels or degrees of acting.

K: All that too is a very small affair. What do you say, Sir?

DB: Well, since the consciousness emerges from the ground, this activity is affecting all mankind from the ground.

K: Yes.

DB: You see many people will find this very difficult to understand.

K: I am not interested in many people. I want to understand you, 'X' and me, 'Y'. That ground, that immensity, is not limited to such a petty little affair. It couldn't be.

DB: The ground includes physically the whole universe.

K: Yes, the whole universe, and to reduce all that to . . .

DB: . . . these little activities . . .

K: . . . is all so silly.

DB: I think that raises the question of what is the significance of mankind in the universe, or in the ground?

K: Yes, that's it.

DB: Because even the best of these little things that we have been doing have very little significance on that scale. Right?

K: Yes, this is just opening the chapter. I think that 'X' is doing something — not doing, but by his very existence . . .

DB: . . . he is making something possible?

K: Yes. When you read of Einstein, he has made something possible, which man hadn't discovered before.

DB: We can see that fairly easily because it works through the usual channels of society.

K: Yes, I understand that. What is 'X' bringing apart from the little things? Putting it into words makes it sound wrong. 'X' has that immense intelligence, that energy, that something, and he must operate at a much greater level than one can possibly conceive, which must affect the consciousness of those who are living in darkness.

DB: Possibly so. The question is, will this effect show in any way? You know, manifestly.

K: Apparently not. If you hear the television or radio news, and know what is happening all over the world, apparently it is not doing so.

DB: That is what is difficult, and a matter of great concern.

K: But it must have an effect. It has to.

DB: Why do you say it has to?

K: Because light must affect darkness.

DB: Perhaps 'Y' might say that, living in darkness, he is not sure that there is such an effect. He might say perhaps there is, but I want to see it manifest. Not seeing anything and still being in darkness, he then asks, what shall I do?

K: I understand that. So are you saying that 'X's' only activity is just writing, teaching etc.?

DB: No. Merely that it may well be that the activity is much greater, but it doesn't show. If only we could see it!

K: How would it be shown? How would 'Y', who wants proof of it, see it?

DB: 'Y' might say something like this: many people have made a similar statement, and some of them have obviously been wrong. But one wants to say it could be true. You see, until now, I think the things we have said make sense, and they follow to a certain extent.

K: Yes, I understand all that.

DB: And now you say something which goes much further. Other people have said things like that and one feels that they were on the wrong track, that they, or at least some of these people, were fooling themselves.

K: No. 'X' says, we are being very logical.

DB: Yes, but at this stage logic will not carry us any further.

K: It is very reasonable! We have been through all that. So 'X's' mind is not acting in an irrational way.

DB: You could say that, having seen the thing was reasonable, so far, 'Y' may have some confidence that it could go further.

K: Yes, that is what I am trying to say.

DB: Of course, there is no proof.

K: No.

DB: So could we explore?

K: That is what I am trying to do.

Q: What about the other activities of 'X'? We said he has the function of teaching, but also that 'X' has other activities.

K: He must have. Necessarily must.

Q: But what?

K: I don't know; we are trying to find that out.

DB: You are saying that somehow he makes possible an activity of the ground in the whole consciousness of mankind which would not have been possible without him.

K: Yes.

Q: His contact with 'Y' is not only verbal. 'Y' listens but there is some other quality . . .

K: Yes, but 'X' says all that is a petty little affair. That is, of course, understood, but 'X' says there is something much greater.

Q: The effect of 'X' is perhaps far greater than can be put in words.

K: We are trying to find out what that greater is that must necessarily be operating.

Q: Is it something that appears in the daily life of 'X'?

K: Yes. In his daily life 'X' is apparently doing fairly small things — teaching, writing, book-keeping, or whatever. But is that all? It seems so silly.

DB: Are you saying that in the daily life 'X' does not look so different from anybody else?

K: No, apparently not.

DB: But there is something else going on which does not show. Right?

K: That's it. When 'X' talks it may be different, he may say things differently but . . .

DB: . . . that is not fundamental, because there are so many people who say things differently from others.

K: I know. But the man who has walked through all that right from the beginning! If such a man has the whole of that energy to call upon, to reduce it all to these petty little things seems ridiculous.

DB: Let me ask a question: Why does the ground require this man to operate on mankind? Why can't the ground, as it were, operate directly on mankind to clear things up?

K: Ah, just a minute, just a minute. Are you asking why the ground demands action?

DB: Why does it require a particular man to affect mankind?

K: Oh, that I can easily explain. It is part of existence, like the stars.

Q: Can the immensity act directly on mankind? Does it have to inform a man to enter the consciousness of mankind?

K: We are talking about something else. I want to find out if 'X' says, I am not going to be reduced only to writing and talking; that is too small and petty. And the other question is, why does the ground need this man? It doesn't need him.

DB: But when he is here, the ground will use him.

K: That is so.

DB: Well, would it be possible that the ground could do something to clear this up?

K: That is what I want to find out. That is why I am saying, in different words, that the ground doesn't need the man, but the man has touched the ground.

DB: Yes.

K: So the ground is using him, let's say employing him. He is part of that movement. Is that all? Do you follow what I mean? Am I asking the wrong questions? Why should he do anything? Except this?

DB: Well, perhaps he does nothing.

K: That very doing nothing, may be the doing.

DB: Doing nothing makes possible the action of the ground. It may be that. In doing nothing which has any specified aim . . .

K: That's right. No specified content which can be translated into human terms.

DB: Yes, but still he is supremely active in doing nothing.

Q: Is there an action which is beyond time, for that man?

K: He is that . . .

Q: Then we cannot ask for a result from that man.

K: He is not asking for results.

Q: But 'Y' is asking for a result.

K: No. Perhaps 'X' says, I am concerned to talk, etc., which is a very small thing. But there is a vast field which must affect the whole of mankind.

DB: There is an analogy which may not be very good but we can consider it. In chemistry, a catalyst makes possible a certain action without itself taking part, but merely by being what it is.

K: Yes, is that what is happening? Even that is a small affair.

DB: Yes.

Q: And even there 'Y' would say it isn't happening, because the world is still in a mess. So is there a truth in the world for the activity of that man?

K: 'X' says he is sorry, but that is no question at all. I am not interested in proving anything. It isn't a mathematical or a technical problem to be shown and proved. 'X' says that he has walked from the beginning of man to the very end of man, and that there is a movement which is timeless. The ground which is the universe, the cosmos, everything. And the ground doesn't need the man, but the man has come upon it. And he is still a man in the world, who says, 'I write and do something or other,' not to prove the ground, not to do anything. 'X' does that just out of compassion. But there is a much greater movement which necessarily plays a part in the world.

Q: Does the greater movement play a part through 'X'?

K: Obviously, 'X' says that there is something else operating which cannot possibly be put into words. He asks, 'What am I to do?' There is nothing which a man like 'Y' will understand. He will immediately translate it into some kind of illusory thing. But 'X' says there is something else. Otherwise it is all so childish.

DB: I think the general view which people are developing now is that the universe has no meaning, that it moves any old way, things just happen, and none of them has any meaning.

K: None of them has meaning for the man who is here, but the man who is there, speaking relatively, says it is full of meaning, and not invented by thought.
    All right, let's leave the vastness, and all that. 'X' says, perhaps there will be ten people with this insight and that might affect society. It will not be communism, socialism, this or that political re-organization. It will be totally different, and based on intelligence and compassion.

DB: Well, if there were ten, they might find a way to spread this much more.

K: That's what I am trying to get at.

DB: What do you mean?

K: 'X' brings the universe, but I translate it into something trivial.

DB: Are you saying that if the whole of mankind were to see this that would be something different?

K: Oh, yes, of course!

DB: Would it be new . . .

K: . . . It would be paradise on earth.

DB: It would be like an organism of a new kind.

K: Of course. But you see, I am not satisfied with this.

DB: Well, what is it?

K: I am not 'satisfied' in leaving this immensity to be reduced to some few words. It seems so stupid, so incredible. You see man, 'Y', is concerned with concepts like 'show me', 'prove it to me', 'what benefit has it?', 'will it affect my future?' You follow? He is concerned with all that. And he is looking at 'X' with eyes that are accustomed to this pettiness! So, he reduces that immensity to his pettiness, and puts it in a temple and has therefore lost it completely. But 'X' says, I won't even look at that; there is something so immense, please do look at it. But 'Y' is always translating it by wanting demonstration, proof or reward. He is always concerned with that. 'X' brings light. That's all he can do. Isn't that enough?

DB: To bring the light which would allow other people to be open to the immensity?

K: Is it like this? We only see a small part, but that very small part extends to infinity?

DB: That small part of what?

K: No. We see immensity only as a very small thing. And that immensity is the whole universe. I can't help but think that it must have some tremendous effect on 'Y'; on society.

DB: Certainly the perception of this *must* have an effect, but it seems that this is not in the consciousness of society at the moment.

K: I know.

DB: But you are saying still the effect is there?

K: Yes.

Q: Are you saying that the perception of even a small part is the infinity?

K: Of course, of course.

Q: Is it in itself the changing factor?

DB: Do you think it is possible that a thing like this could divert the course of mankind away from the dangerous path it is taking?

K: Yes, that is what I think. But to divert the course of man's destruction somebody must listen. Right? Somebody — ten people — must listen!

DB: Yes.

K: Listen to that immensity calling.

DB: So the immensity may divert the course of man. The individual cannot do it.

K: Yes. The individual cannot do it, obviously. But 'X' who is supposed to be an individual, has trodden this path, and says, 'Listen'. But man does not listen.

DB: Well, then, is it possible to discover how to make people listen?

K: No, then we are back!

DB: What do you mean?

K: Don't act; you have nothing to do.

DB: What does it mean not to do a thing?

K: I realize, as 'Y', that whatever I do — whether I sacrifice, practise, renounce — whatever I do, I am still living in that circle of darkness. So 'X' says, 'Don't act; you have nothing to do.' You follow? But that is translated by 'Y', who does everything except wait and see what happens. We must pursue this, Sir, otherwise it is all so hopeless from the point of view of 'Y'.

19 APRIL 1980, OJAI, CALIFORNIA

NINE

Senility and the Brain Cells

KRISHNAMURTI: I would like to talk over with you, and perhaps with Narayan* too, what is happening to the human brain. We have a civilization that is highly cultivated, and yet at the same time barbarous, with selfishness clothed in all kinds of spiritual garbs. Deep down, however, there is a frightening selfishness. Man's brain has been evolving through millenia upon millenia, yet it has come to this divisive, destructive point, which we all know. So I am wondering whether the human brain — not a particular brain, but the human brain — is deteriorating? Whether it is just in a slow and steady decline? Or whether it is possible in one's life-time to bring about in the brain a total renewal from all this; a renewal that will be pristine, original, unpolluted? I have been wondering about this, and I would like to discuss it.

I think the human brain is not a particular brain; it doesn't belong to me, or to anyone else. It is the human brain which has evolved over millions of years. And in that evolution it has gathered tremendous experience, knowledge and all the cruelties, vulgarities and brutalities of selfishness. Is there a possibility of its sloughing off all this, and becoming something else? Because apparently it is functioning in patterns. Whether it is a religious pattern, a scientific, a business, or a family pattern, it is always operating, functioning in small narrow circles. Those circles are clashing against each other, and there seems to be no end to this. So what will break down this forming of patterns, so that there is no falling into other new patterns, but breaking down the whole system of patterns, whether pleasant or unpleasant? After all, the brain has had many shocks, challenges and pressures upon it, and if it is not capable of renewing or rejuvenating itself, there is very little hope. You follow?

DAVID BOHM: You see, one difficulty might present itself. If you are thinking of the brain structure, we cannot get into the structure, physically.

*Mr G. Narayan, Principal of the Rishi Valley School in India.

K: Physically we cannot. I know, we have discussed this. So what is the brain to do? The brain specialists can look at it, take the dead brain of a human being and examine it, but it doesn't solve the problem. Right?

DB: No.

K: So what is a human being to do, knowing it cannot be changed from outside? The scientist, the brain specialist and the neurologist explain various things but their explanations, their investigations, are not going to solve this.

DB: Well, there is no evidence that they can.

K: No evidence.

DB: Some people who do bio-feedback think that they can influence the brain, connecting an instrument to the electrical potentials in the skull and being able to look at them; you can also change your heart beat and blood pressure and other things. These people have raised the hope that something could be done.

K: But they are not succeeding.

DB: They are not getting very far.

K: And we can't wait for these scientists and bio-feedbackers — sorry! — to solve the problem. So what shall we do?

DB: The next question is whether the brain can be aware of its own structure.

K: Can the brain be aware of its own movement? And can the brain not only be aware of its own movement, but itself have enough energy to break all patterns and move out of them?

DB: You have to ask to what extent the brain is free to break out of patterns?

K: What do you mean?

DB: Well, you see, if you begin by saying that the brain is caught in a pattern, it may not be so.

K: But apparently it is.

DB: As far as we can see. It may not be free to break out. It may not have the power.

K: That is what I have said: not enough energy, not enough power.

DB: Yes, it may not be able to take the action needed to get out.

K: So it has become its own prisoner. Then what?

DB: Then that is the end.

K: *Is* that the end?

DB: If that is true, then that is the end. If the brain cannot break out then perhaps people would choose to try some other way to solve the problem.

NARAYAN: When we speak of the brain, in one sense it is connected to the senses and the nervous system; the feed-back is there. Is there another instrument to which the brain is connected which has a different effect on the brain?

K: What do you mean by that? Some other factor?

N: Some other factor in the human system itself. Because, obviously, through the senses the brain does get nourishment, but still that is not enough. Is there some other internal factor which gives energy to the brain?

K: You see, I want to discuss this. The brain is constantly occupied with various problems, with holding on, attachment, and so on. It is constantly in a state of preoccupation. That may be the central factor. And, if it is not in occupation, does it go sluggish? If it is not occupied, can it maintain the energy that is required to break down the patterns?

DB: Now the first point is that if the brain is not occupied, somebody might think that it would just take things easy.

K: Become lazy and all that! I don't mean that.

DB: If you mean not occupied, but still active . . .

K: Of course. I mean that.

DB: Then we have to go into what is the nature of the activity.

K: Yes. This brain is so occupied with conflicts, struggles, attachments, fears and pleasures. And this occupation gives to the brain its own energy. If it is not occupied, will it become lazy, drugged, and so lose its elasticity, as it were? Or will that unoccupied state give the brain the required energy to break the patterns?

DB: What makes you say this might happen? We were discussing the other day that when the brain is kept busy with intellectual activity and thought, it does not decay and shrink.

K: As long as it is thinking, moving, living.

DB: Thinking in a rational way; then it remains strong.

K: Yes. That is what I want to get at too. Which is, as long as it is functioning, moving, thinking rationally . . .

DB: . . . it remains strong. If it starts irrational movement, then it breaks down. Also if it gets caught in a routine it begins to die.

K: That's it. If the brain is caught in any routine — the meditation routine, or the routine of the priests.

DB: Or the daily life of the farmer . . .

K: . . . the farmer, etc., it must gradually become dull.

DB: Not only that, but it seems to shrink.

K: To shrink physically.

DB: Perhaps some of the cells die?

K: To shrink physically, and the opposite to that is the eternal occupation with business — by anyone who does a routine job . . . thinking, thinking, thinking! And we believe that that also prevents shrinking.

DB: Surely experience seems to show that it does, from measurements that have been made.

K: Yes, it does. That's it.

DB: The brain starts to shrink at a certain age. Now that is what they have discovered, and just as when the body is not being used the muscles begin to lose their flexibility . . .

K: So, take lots of exercise!

DB: Well, they say exercise the body and exercise the brain.

K: Yes. If it is caught in any pattern, any routine, any directive, it must shrink.

DB: Could we go into what makes it shrink?

K: That is fairly simple. It is repetition.

DB: Repetition is mechanical, and doesn't really use the full capacity of the brain.

K: One has noticed that people who have spent years and years in meditation are the most dull people on earth. And also with lawyers and professors there is ample evidence of all that.

N: It is suggested that rational thinking postpones senility. But rational thinking itself can sometimes become a pattern.

DB: It might. Rational thinking pursued in a narrow area might become part of the pattern too.

K: Of course, of course.

DB: But is there some other way?

K: We will go into that.

DB: But let's clear up things about the body first. You see, if somebody does a lot of exercise for the body, it remains strong, but it can become mechanical.

K: Yes.

DB: And therefore it would have a bad effect.

N: What about the various traditional religious instruments — yoga, tantra, kundalini, etc.?

K: I know. Oh, they must shrink! Because of what is happening. Take yoga for example. It used not to be vulgarized, if I may use that word. It was kept strictly to the very few, who were not concerned about kundalini and all that, but who were concerned with leading a moral, ethical, so-called spiritual life. You see, I want to get at the root of this.

DB: I think there is something related to this. It seems that before man was organized into society, he was living close to nature, and it was not possible to live in a routine.

K: No, it was not.

DB: But it was completely insecure.

K: So we are saying that the brain itself becomes extraordinarily alive — is not caught in a pattern — if it lives in a state of uncertainty? Without becoming neurotic!

DB: I think that is more clear when you say not becoming neurotic — then certainty becomes a form of neurosis. But I would rather that the brain lives without having certainty, without demanding it, without demanding certain knowledge.

K: So are we saying that knowledge also withers the brain?

DB: Yes, when it is repetitious and becomes mechanical.

K: But knowledge itself?

DB: Well, we have to be very careful there. I think that knowledge has a tendency to become mechanical. That is, it gets fixed, but we could always be learning, you see.

K: But learning from a centre, learning as an accumulative process!

DB: Learning with something fixed. You see, we learn something as fixed, and then you learn from there. If we were to be learning without holding anything permanently fixed . . .

K: Learning and not adding. Can we do that?

DB: Yes, I think to a certain extent we have to drop our knowledge. You see, knowledge may be valid up to a point, and then it ceases to be valid. It gets in the way. You could say that our civilization is collapsing because of too much knowledge.

K: Of course.

DB: We don't discard what is in the way.

N: Many forms of knowledge are additive. Unless you know the previous thing, you can't do the next thing. Would you say that kind of knowledge is repetitive?

DB: No. As long as we are learning. But if we hold some principle, or the centre, fixed, and say it cannot change, then that knowledge becomes mechanical. But, for example, suppose you have to make a living. People must organize society, and so on, and they need knowledge.

K: But there we add more and more.

DB: That's right. We may also get rid of some.

K: Of course.

DB: Some gets in the way, you see. It is continually moving there.

K: Yes, but I am asking, apart from that, about knowledge itself.

DB: Do you mean knowledge without this content?

K: Yes; the knowing mind.

DB: Mind which merely wants knowledge, is that what you are saying? Knowledge for its own sake?

K: Yes. I want to question the whole idea of having knowledge.

DB: But, again, it is not too clear, because we accept that we need some knowledge.

K: Of course, at a certain level.

DB: So it is not clear what kind of knowledge it is that you are questioning.

K: I am questioning the experience that leaves knowledge, that leaves a mark.

DB: Yes, but what kind of mark? A psychological mark?

K: Psychological, of course.

DB: You are questioning this, rather than knowledge of technique and matter, and so on. But you see, when you use the word knowledge by itself, it tends to include the whole.

K: We have said that knowledge at a certain level is essential; there you can add and take away and keep on changing. But I am questioning whether psychological knowledge is not in itself a factor of the shrinking of the brain.

DB: What do you mean by psychological knowledge? Knowledge about the mind, knowledge about myself?

K: Yes. Knowledge about myself, and living in that knowledge, and accumulating that knowledge.

DB: So if you keep on accumulating knowledge about yourself or about relationships . . .

K: . . . yes, about relationships. That's it. Would you say such knowledge helps the brain, or makes the brain somewhat inactive, makes it shrink?

DB: Brings it into a rut.

K: Yes.

DB: But one should see what it is about this knowledge that makes trouble.

K: What is this knowlege that makes so much trouble? In relationship, that knowledge creates trouble.

DB: Yes, it gets in the way because it fixes.

K: If I have an image about someone, that knowledge is obviously going to impede our relationship. It becomes a pattern.

DB: Yes, the knowledge about myself and about him and how we are related, makes a pattern.

K: And therefore that becomes a routine and so it loses its energy.

DB: Yes, and it occurred to me that routine in that area is more dangerous than routine in, say, the area of daily work.

K: That's right.

DB: And if routine in ordinary work can shrink the brain, then in that area it might do some worse thing, because it has a bigger effect.

K: Can the brain, in psychological matters, be entirely free from this kind of knowledge? Look! I am a businessman, and get into the car, bus, taxi or tube train, and I am thinking about what I am going to do, whom I am going to meet in connection with business. My mind is all the time living in that area. Then I come home; there is my wife and children; sex and all that. That also becomes a psychological knowledge from which I am acting. So there is the knowledge of my business, and also the knowledge with regard to my wife and my reactions in relationship. These two are in contradiction, unless I am unaware of them, and just carry on. If I *am* aware of these two, it becomes a disturbing factor.

DB: Also people find that this is a routine. They get bored with it, and they begin to . . .

K: . . . divorce, and then the whole circus begins!

DB: They may hope that by becoming occupied with something else they will get out of their boredom.

K: Yes, by going to church, etc. Any escape is an occupation. So I am asking whether this psychological knowledge is not a factor of the shrinkage of the brain?

DB: Well, it could be a factor.

K: It *is*.

DB: If knowledge of your profession or skill can be a factor, then this psychological knowledge is stronger.

K: Of course. Much stronger.

N: When you say psychological knowledge you are making a distinction between psychological knowledge and, let us say, scientific knowledge or factual knowledge?

K: Of course, we have said that.

N: But I am a little wary of the claim that scientific knowledge and other types of factual knowledge help to extend the brain, to make it bigger. That in itself doesn't lead anywhere. Though it postpones energy.

K: Dr. Bohm makes this very clear. Rational thinking becomes merely routine; I think logically, and therefore I have learned the trick of that, but I keep on repeating it.

N: That is what happens in most forms of rational thinking.

K: Of course.

DB: I think that there is a dependence on being faced with continual problems.

K: Of course.

DB: You see, lawyers may feel that their brains will last longer, because they are presented with constantly different problems, and therefore they cannot think entirely according to routine!

K: But, just a minute! They may have different clients with different problems, but they are acting from fixed knowledge.

DB: They would not say entirely, they have got to find new facts, and so on.

K: They are not functioning entirely in routine but the basis is knowledge — precedence and book knowledge and experience with various clients.

DB: But then you would have to say that some other more subtle degeneration of the brain takes place, not merely shrinkage.

K: That's right. That's what I want to get at.

DB: You see, when a baby is born, the brain cells have very few cross connections; these gradually increase in number, and then, as a person approaches senility, they begin to go back. So the quality of those cross connections could be wrong. If, for example, we repeated them too often, they would get too fixed.

N: Are all the brain functions confined to rational forms, or are there some functions which have a different quality?

DB: Well, it is known that a large part of the brain deals with movement of the body, with muscles, with various organs and so on, and this part does not shrink with age, although the part that deals with rational thought, if it is not used, does shrink. Then there may be other functions that are totally unknown; that is, very little is actually known about the brain.

K: What we are saying is that we are only using one part of the brain. There is only partial activity, partial occupation, either rational or irrational. But as long as the brain is occupied it must be in that limited area. Would you say that?

DB: Then what will happen when it is not occupied? We can say that it may tend to spend most of the time occupied in the limited set of functions which are mechanical, and that this will produce some subtle degeneration of the brain tissue, since anything like that will affect the brain tissue.

K: Are we saying that senility is the result of a mechanical way of living? Of mechanical knowledge, so that the brain has no freedom, no space?

DB: That is the suggestion. It is not necessarily accepted by all the people who work on the brain. They have shown that the brain cells start to die around the age of thirty or forty at a steady rate, but this may be a factor. I don't think their measurements are so good that they can test effectively how the brain is used. You see, they are merely rough measurements, made statistically. But you want to propose that this death or degeneration of the brain cells comes from the wrong way of using the brain?

K: That's right. That is what I am trying to get at.

DB: Yes, and there is a little bit of evidence from the scientists, although I think that they don't know very much about it.

K: You see, scientists, brain specialists, are, if I may put it simply, examining things outside, but not taking themselves as guinea-pigs, and not going into that.

DB: Mostly, you see, except for those who do bio-feedback, they are trying to work on themselves in a very indirect way.

K: Yes, but I feel we haven't time for all that.

DB: It is too slow, and it isn't very deep.

K: So let's come back to the realization that any activity which is repeated, which is directed in the narrow sense, any method, any routine, logical or illogical, *does* affect the brain. We have understood that very clearly. Knowledge at a certain level is essential, but psychological knowledge about oneself, one's experiences, etc. becomes routine. The images I have about myself also obviously become routine, and all that helps to bring about a shrinkage of the brain. I have understood all that very clearly. And any kind of occupation, apart from the mechanical . . . no, not mechanical . . .

DB: . . . physical.

K: . . . apart from physical occupation, brings about shrinkage of the brain. Now how is this process to stop? And if it does stop, will there be a renewal?

DB: I think that some brain scientists would doubt that the brain cells could be renewed, and I don't know that there is any proof one way or the other.

K: I think they can be renewed. That is what I want to get at.

DB: So we have to discuss that.

N: Are you implying that mind is different from the brain, that mind is distinct from the brain?

K: Not quite.

DB: You have spoken of universal mind.

N: Mind, in the sense that one has access to this mind, and it is not the brain. Do you consider that a possibility?

K: I don't quite follow this. I would say that the mind is all-inclusive. When it is all-inclusive, of brain, emotions — all that; when it is totally whole, not divisive in itself, there is a quality which is universal. Right?

N: One has access to it?

K: Not one: no, you can't reach it. You can't say, I have access to it.

N: I am only saying access. One doesn't possess it, but . . .

K: You can't possess the sky!

N: No, my point is, is there a way of being open to it and is there a function of the mind through which the whole of it can become accessible?

K: I think there is. We may come to that presently if we can stick to this point: We are asking now, can the brain renew itself, rejuvenate, become young again without any shrinkage at all? I think it can. I want to open a new chapter and discuss this. Psychologically, knowledge that man has acquired is crippling it. The Freudians, the Jungians, the latest psychologist, the latest psycho-therapist, are all helping to make the brain shrink. Sorry! I don't mean to give offence. . . .

N: Is there a way of forgetting this knowledge then?

K: No, no. Not forgetting. I see what psychological knowledge is doing and I see the waste; I see what is taking place if I follow that line. It is obvious. So I don't follow that avenue at all. I discard analysis altogether. That is a pattern we have learnt, not only from the recent psychologists and psycho-therapists but also through the tradition of a million years of analysis, of introspect, or of saying, 'I must', and 'I must not', 'This is right and that is wrong'. You know the whole process. I personally don't do it, and so I reject that whole method.

We are coming to a point, which is direct perception and immediate action. Our perception is generally directed by knowledge, by the past, which is knowledge perceiving, and with action arising, acting from that. This is a factor of shrinking of the brain, of senility.

Is there a perception which is *not* time binding? And so action which is immediate? Am I making myself clear? That is, as long as the brain, which has evolved through time, is still living in a pattern of time, it is becoming senile. If we could break that pattern of time, the brain has broken out of its pattern, and therefore something else takes place.

N: How does the brain break out of the pattern of time?

K: We will come to that, but first let's see if we agree.

DB: Well, you are saying that the brain is the pattern of time, and perhaps this should be clarified. I think that what you mean by analysis is some sort of process based on past knowledge, which organizes our perception, and in which we take a series of steps to try to accumulate knowledge about the whole thing. And now you say that this is a pattern of time, and we have to break out of it.

K: If we agree that this is so, the brain is functioning in a pattern of time.

DB: Then we have to ask, what other pattern is possible?

K: But wait . . .

DB: What other movement is possible?

K: No. First let's understand this, not merely verbally, but let's actually see that it is happening. That our action, our way of living, our whole thinking, is bound by time, or comes with the knowledge of time.

DB: Certainly our thinking about ourselves, any attempt to analyse ourselves, to think about ourselves, involves this process.

K: This process, which is of time. Right?

N: That is a difficulty: when you say knowledge and experience, they are a certain cohesive energy or force that binds you.

K: Which means what? Time binding!

N: Time binding and . . .

K: . . . and therefore the pattern of centuries, of millenia, is being repeated.

N: Yes. But I am saying that this has a certain cohesive force.

K: Of course, of course. All illusions have an extraordinary vitality.

N: Very few break through.

K: Look at all the churches and what immense vitality they have.

N: No, apart from these churches, one's personal life, it has a certain cohesive force that keeps one back. One can't break away from it.

K: What do you mean, it keeps you back?

N: It has a magnetic attraction, it sort of pulls you back. You can't free yourself of it unless you have some instrument with which you can act.

K: We are going to find out if there is a different approach to the problem.

DB: When you say, a different instrument, that is not clear. The whole notion of an instrument involves time, because if you use any instrument, it is a process which you plan.

K: Time; that's just it.

N: That is why I use the word 'instrument'; I mean, it is effective.

K: It has not been effective. On the contrary, it is destructive. So do I see the very truth of its destructiveness? Not just the theory, the idea, but the actuality of it. If I do, then what takes place? The brain has evolved through time, and has been functioning, living, acting, believing in that time process. But when one realizes that all this helps to make the brain senile, when one sees that as true, then what is the next step?

N: Are you implying that the very seeing that it is destructive is a releasing factor?

K: Yes.

N: And there is no need for an extra instrument?

K: No. Don't use the word instrument.
    There is no other factor. We are concerned to end this shrinkage and senility, and in asking whether the brain itself, the cells, the whole thing, can move out of time? I am not talking about immortality, and all that kind of stuff! Can the brain move out of time altogether? Otherwise deterioration, shrinkage and senility are inevitable, and even when senility may not show, the brain cells are becoming weaker, and so on.

N: If the brain cells are material and physical, somehow or other they have to shrink through time; indeed it can't be helped. The brain cell, which is tissue, cannot in physical terms be immortal.

DB: Perhaps the rate of shrinkage would be greatly slowed down. If a person lives a certain number of years, and his brain begins to shrink long before he dies, then he becomes senile. Now if the deterioration would slow then . . .

K: . . . not only slown down, Sir.

DB: . . . Well, regenerate . . .

K: . . . be in a state of non-occupation.

DB: I think Narayan is saying that it is impossible for any material system to last for ever.

K: I am not talking about lasting for ever — though I am not sure if it can't last for ever! No, this is very serious, I am not pulling anybody's leg.

DB: If all the cells were to regenerate in the body and in the brain, then the whole thing could go on indefinitely.

K: Look, we are now destroying the body, through drink, smoking, over-indulgence in sex and all kinds of things. We are living most unhealthily. Right? If the body were in excellent health, maintained right through — which means no heightened emotions, no strain, no sense of deterioration, the heart functioning normally — then why not?

DB: Well . . .

K: . . . which means what? No travelling, and all the rest of it. . . .

DB: No excitement.

K: If the body remains in one quiet place I am sure it can last a great many more years than it does now.

DB: Yes, I think that is true. There have been many cases of people living for a hundred and fifty years in quiet places. I think that is all you are talking about. You are not really suggesting something lasting for ever?

K: So the body can be kept healthy, and since the body affects the mind, nerves, senses and all that, they also can be kept healthy.

DB: And if the brain is kept in the right action . . .

K: . . . yes, without any strain.

DB: You see the brain has a tremendous affect on organizing the body. The pituitary gland controls the entire system of the body glands; also all the organs of the body are controlled by the brain. When the mind deteriorates, the body starts to deteriorate.

K: Of course.

DB: They work together.

K: They go together. So can this brain — which is not 'my' brain — which has evolved through millions of years, which has had all kinds of destructive or pleasant experiences . . .

DB: You mean it is a typical brain, not a particular brain, peculiar to some individual? When you say 'not mine', you mean any brain belonging to mankind, right?

K: Any brain.

DB: They are all basically similar.

K: Similar: that is what I said. Can that brain be free of all this? Of time? I think it can.

DB: Perhaps we could discuss what it means to be free of time. You see, at first the suggestion that the brain be free of time might sound crazy, but, obviously, we all know that you don't mean that the clock stops.

K: Science fiction and all that!

DB: The point is, what does it really mean to be psychologically free of time?

K: That there is no tomorrow.

DB: But we know there *is* tomorrow.

K: But psychologically . . .

DB: Can you describe better, what you mean when you say 'no tomorrow'?

K: What does it mean to be living in time? Let's take the other side first, because then we come to the other. What does it mean to live in time? Hope; thinking and living in the past, and acting from the knowledge of the past; images, illusions, prejudices — they are all an outcome of the past. All that is time, and that is producing chaos in the world.

DB: Well, suppose we say that if we are not living psychologically in time, we may still order our actions by the watch. The thing that is puzzling is if somebody says, I am not living in time, but I must keep an appointment. You see?

K: Of course; you can't sit here for ever.

DB: So you say, I am looking at the watch, but I am not psychologically extending how I am going to feel in the next hour, when I have fulfilment of desire, etc.

K: I am just saying that the way we are living now is in the field of time. And there we have brought all kinds of problems and suffering. Is that right?

DB: Yes, but it should be made clear why this necessarily produces suffering. You are saying that if you live in the field of time suffering is inevitable.

K: Inevitable.

DB: Why?

K: It is simple. Time has built the ego, the 'me', the image of me sustained by society, by education, which has built through millions of years. All that is the result of time. And from there I act.

N: Yes.

DB: Towards the future psychologically; that is, towards some future state of being.

K: Yes. Which means that the centre is always becoming.

DB: Trying to become better.

K: Better, nobler, or anything else. So all that, the constant endeavour to become something psychologically, is a factor of time.

DB: Are you saying that the endeavour to become produces suffering?

K: Obviously. It is simple. All that is divisive. It divides me from others, and so you are different from me. And when I depend on somebody, and that somebody is gone, I feel lonely and miserable. All that goes on.
    So we are saying that any factor of division, which is the very nature of the self, must inevitably cause suffering.

DB: Are you saying that through time the self is set up, and then the self introduces division and conflict and so on? But that if there were no psychological time, then perhaps this entire structure would collapse, and something entirely different would happen?

K: That's it. That is what I am saying. And therefore the brain itself has broken up.

DB: Well, that is the next step — to say that the brain has broken out of that rut, and perhaps could then regenerate. It doesn't follow logically, but still it could be so.

K: I think it does follow logically.

DB: Well, it follows logically that it would stop degenerating.

K: Yes.

DB: And are you adding further that it would start to regenerate?

K: You look sceptical?

N: Yes, because the whole human predicament is bound to time.

K: We know that.

N: Society, individuals, the whole structure.

K: I know, I know.

N: It is so forceful that anything feeble doesn't work here.

K: What do you mean — 'feeble'?

N: The force of this is so great that what has to break through must have tremendous energy.

K: Yes.

N: And no individual seems to be able to generate sufficient energy to be able to break through.

K: But you have got hold of the wrong end of the stick, if I may point this out. When you use the word 'individual', you have moved away from the fact that our brain is universal.

N: Yes, I admit that.

K: There is no individuality.

N: That brain is conditioned this way.

K: Yes, we have been through all that. It is conditioned this way through time. Time is conditioning — right? It is not that time has created the conditioning, time itself is the factor of conditioning.

So can that time element *not* exist? (We are talking about psychological time, not the ordinary physical time.) I say it can. We have said that the ending of suffering comes about when the self, which is built up through time, is no longer there. A man who is actually going through agony might reject this. But when he comes out of the shock of it, if somebody points out to him what is happening, and if he is willing to listen, to see the rationality, the sanity of it, and not to build a wall against it, he is out of that field. The brain is out of that time-binding quality.

N: Temporarily.

K: Ah! There again when you use the word 'temporary', it means time.

N: No, I mean that the man slips back into time.

K: No, he can't. He can't go back if he sees that something is dangerous, like a cobra, or any other danger, he cannot go back to it.

N: That analogy is a bit difficult, because the structure itself is that danger. One inadvertently slips into it.

K: When you see a dangerous animal, there is immediate action. It may be the result of past knowledge and experience, but there is immediate action for self-protection. But psychologically we are unaware of the dangers. If we become as aware of these dangers as we are aware of physical dangers, there is an action which is not time-binding.

DB: Yes, I think you could say that as long as you could perceive this danger you know you would respond immediately. But you see, if you were to use that analogy of the animal, it might be an animal that you realize is dangerous, but he might take another form that you *don't* see as dangerous!

K: Yes.

DB: Therefore there would be a danger of slipping back if you didn't see this. Or illusion might come in some other form.

K: Of course.

DB: But I think the major point you are making is that the brain is not belonging to any individual.

K: Yes, absolutely.

DB: And therefore it is no use saying that the individual slips back.

K: No.

DB: Because that already denies what you are saying. The danger is rather that the brain might slip back.

K: The brain itself might slip back, because it has not seen the danger.

DB: It hasn't seen the other forms of the illusions.

K: The Holy Ghost taking different shapes! All this is the real root of time.

DB: Time, and separation as individuality, are basically the same structure.

K: Of course.

DB: Although it is not obvious in the beginning.

K: I wonder if we see that.

DB: It might be worth discussing that. Why is psychological time the same illusion, the same structure as individuality? Individuality is the sense of being a person who is located here somewhere.

K: Located and divided.

DB: Divided from the others. He extends out to some periphery, his domain extends out to some periphery, and also he has an identity which extends over time. He wouldn't regard himself as an individual if he said 'Today I am one person, tomorrow I am another'. So it seems that we mean by individual somebody who is in time.

K: I think that this idea of individuality is a fallacy.

DB: Yes, but many people may find it hard to be convinced that it is a fallacy. There is a common feeling that, as an individual, I have existed at least from my birth if not before, and go on to death, and perhaps later. The whole idea of being an individual is to be in time. Right?

K: Obviously.

DB: To be in psychological time, not just the time of the clock.

K: Yes, we are saying that. So can that illusion that time has created individuality be broken? Can this brain understand that?

DB: I think that, as Narayan said, there is a great momentum in the brain, which keeps rolling, moving along.

K: Can that momentum stop?

N: The difficulty comes here. The genetic coding is intrinsic to a person. He seems to function more or less unconsciously, driven by this past momentum. And suddenly he sees, like a flash, something true. But the difficulty is that it may operate only for a day — and then he is again caught in the old momentum.

K: I know that. But it says the brain will not be caught. Once the mind or the brain is aware of this fact, it cannot go back. How can it?

N: There must be another way of preventing it from going back.

K: Not preventing: that means also time. You are still thinking in terms of prevention.

N: Prevention, in the sense of the human factor.

K: The human being is irrational. Right? And as long as he is functioning irrationally, he says of any rational factor, 'I refuse to see it'.

N: You are suggesting that the very seeing prevents you from slipping back. This is a human condition.

DB: I wonder if we should go further into this question about prevention. It may be important.

N: There are two aspects. You see the fallacy of something, and the very seeing prevents you from slipping back, because you see the danger of it.

DB: In another sense you say you have no temptation to slip back, therefore you don't have to be prevented. If you really see it, there is no need for conscious prevention.

N: Then you are not tempted to go back.

K: I can't go back. If for example I see the fallacy of all the religious nonsense, it is finished!

DB: The only question which I raise is that you may not see this so completely in another form.

N: It may come in different shapes . . .

DB: . . . and then you are tempted once again.

K: The mind is aware, it is not caught. But you are saying that it is.

N: Yes, in other shapes and forms.

K: Wait Sir. We have said that perception is out of time, is seeing immediately the whole nature of time. Which to use a good old word, is to have an insight into the nature of time. If there is that insight, the very brain cells, which are part of time, break down. The brains cells bring about a change in themselves. You may disagree, you may say, 'Prove it.' I say this is not a matter of proof, it is a matter of action. Do it, find out, test it.

N: You were also saying the other day, that when the consciousness is empty of its content . . .

K: . . . the content being time . . .

N: . . . that leads to the transformation of the brain cells.

K: Yes.

N: When you say consciousness is empty of the content there . . .

K: . . . there is no consciousness as we know it.

N: Yes. And you are using the word insight. What is the connection between the two?

DB: Between what?

N: Consciousness and insight. You have suggested that when consciousness is empty of its content . . .

K: Be careful. Consciousness is put together by its content. The content is the result of time.

DB: The content also *is* time.

K: Of course.

DB: It is about time as well, and it is actually put together by time, also it is about time. But if you have an insight into that, the whole pattern is gone, broken. The insight is not of time, not of memory, is not of knowledge.

N: Who has this insight?

K: Not 'who'. Simply, there is an insight.

N: There is an insight and then the consciousness is empty of its content . . .

K: No, Sir. No.

N: You are implying that the very emptying of the content is insight?

K: No. We are saying time is a factor which has made up the content. It has built it up, and it also thinks about it. All that bundle is the result of time. Insight into this whole movement, which is not 'my' insight, brings about transformations in the brain. Because that insight is not time-binding.

DB: Are you saying that this psychological content is a certain structure, physically, in the brain? That in order for this psychological content to exist, the brain over many years has made many connections of the cells, which constitute this content?

K: Quite, quite.

DB: And then there is a flash of insight, which sees all this, and that it is not necessary. Therefore all this begins to dissipate. And when it has dissipated, there is no content. Then, whatever the brain does is something different.

K: Let us go further. Then there is total emptiness.

DB: Well, emptiness of the content. But when you say total emptiness, you mean emptiness of all this inward content?

K: That's right. And that emptiness has tremendous energy. It *is* energy.

DB: So could you say that the brain, having had all these connections tangled, has locked up a lot of energy?

K: That's right. Wastage of energy.

DB: And when they begin to dissipate, that energy is there.

K: Yes.

DB: Would you say that it is as much physical energy as any other kind?

K: Of course. Now we can go on in more detail, but is this principle, the root of it, an idea or a fact? I hear all this physically with the ear, but I may make it into an idea. If I hear it, not only with the ear, but in my being, in the very structure of myself, what happens then? If that kind of hearing doesn't take place, all this becomes merely an idea, and I spin along for the rest of my life playing with ideas.

If there was a scientist here, bio-feedback or another brain specialist, would he accept all this? Would he even listen to it?

DB: A few scientists would, but obviously the majority would not.

K: No. So how do we touch the human brain?

DB: All this will sound rather abstract, to most scientists, you see. They will say, it could be so; it is a nice theory, but we have no proof of it.

K: Of course. They would say it doesn't excite them very much because they don't see any proof.

DB: They would say, if you have some more evidence we will come back later, and become very interested. So you see, you can't give any proof, because whatever is happening, nobody can see it with their eyes.

K: I understand. But I am asking, what shall we do? The human brain — not 'my' brain or 'your', the brain — has evolved through a million years. One biological 'freak' can move out of it, but how do you get at the human mind generally to make it see all this?

DB: I think you have to communicate the necessity, the inevitability of what you are saying. Say if a person sees something happening before his eyes he says, 'That's so'. Right?

K: But it requires somebody to listen, somebody who says, 'I want to capture it, I want to understand this, I want to find out.' You follow what I am saying? Apparently that is one of the most difficult things in life.

DB: Well, it is the function of this occupied brain — that it is occupied with itself and it doesn't listen.

N: In fact one of the things is that this occupation starts very early. When you are young it is very powerful, and it continues all through your life. How can we, through education, make this clear?

K: The moment you see the importance of not being occupied — see that as a tremendous truth — you will find ways and methods to help educationally, creatively. No one can be told, copy and imitate, for then he is lost.

DB: Then the question is, how is it possible to communicate to the brain, which rejects, which doesn't listen? Is there a way?

K: Not if I refuse to listen. You see, I think meditation is a great factor in all this. I feel we have been meditating although ordinarily people wouldn't accept this as meditation.

DB: They have used the word so often . . .

K: . . . that its meaning is really lost. But true meditation is this: the emptying of consciousness. You follow?

DB: Yes, but let's be clear. Earlier you said it would happen through insight. Now are you saying that meditation is conducive to insight?

K: Meditation *is* insight.

DB: It is insight already. Then is it some sort of work you do? Insight is usually thought of as the flash, but meditation is more constant.

K: We must be careful. What do we mean by meditation? We can reject the systems, methods, acknowledged authorities, because these are often merely traditional repetitions — time-binding nonsense.

N: Do you think some of them could have been original, could have had real insight, in the past?

K: Who knows? Now meditation is this penetration, this sense of moving without any past.

DB: The only point to clear up is that when you use the word meditation, you mean something more than insight, you see.

K: Much more. Insight has freed the brain from the past, from time. That is an enormous statement . . .

DB: Do you mean that you have to have insight if you are going to meditate?

K: Yes, that's right. To meditate without any sense of becoming.

DB: You cannot meditate without insight. You can't regard it as a procedure by which you will come to insight.

K: No. That immediately implies time. A procedure, a system, a method, in order to have insight is nonsensical. Insight into greed or fear frees the mind from them. Then meditation has quite a different quality. It has nothing to do with all the gurus' meditations. So could we say that to have insight there must be silence?

DB: Well, that is the same; we seem to be going in a circle.

K: For the moment.

DB: Yes, my mind has silence.

K: So the silence of insight has cleansed, purged, all that.

DB: All that structure of the occupation.

K: Yes. Then there is no movement as we know it; no movement of time.

DB: Is there movement of some other kind?

K: I don't see how we can measure that by words, that sense of a limitless state.

DB: But you were saying earlier that nevertheless it is necessary to find some language, even though it is unsayable!

K: Yes — we will find that language.

1 June 1980, Brockwood Park, Hampshire

TEN

Cosmic Order

KRISHNAMURTI: We left off the other day by saying that when the mind is totally empty of all the things that thought has put there, then real meditation begins. But I would like to go more deeply into that matter, to go back a bit, and find out if the mind, the brain, can ever be free from all illusion and forms of deception. Also whether it can have its own order — an order not introduced by thought, effort or any endeavour to put things in their proper place. And also, however much damaged the brain is by shock and all kinds of situations, whether it can heal itself completely.

So first let's begin by asking if there is an order which is not made by man or by thought — which is not the result of calculated order out of disturbance, and therefore still part of the old conditioning?

DAVID BOHM: Are you referring to the mind? I mean, you can say the order of nature exists on its own.

K: The order of nature is order.

DB: Yes, it is not made by man.

K: But I am not talking of such. I am not sure that it is that kind of order. Is there cosmic order?

DB: Well, that is still the same thing, in a sense, because the word 'cosmos' means order, but the whole order, which includes the order of the universe and the order of the mind.

K: Yes. What I am trying to find out is whether there is order which man can never possibly conceive?

DB: Well, how are we going to discuss it?

K: I don't know. What is order?

NARAYAN: There is mathematical order, the highest kind of order known to any discipline.

K: Would the mathematicians agree that mathematics is complete order?

N: Yes, mathematics itself is order.

DB: I think it depends on the mathematician. But there is a well-known mathematician called von Neumann who defined mathematics as the relationship of relationships. Really he meant, by relationship, order. It is order working within the field of order itself, rather than working on some object.

K: Yes, that is what I am trying to get at.

DB: So the most creative mathematicians are having a perception of this, which may be called pure order; but of course it is limited, because it has to be expressed mathematically, in terms of formulae or equations.

K: Of course. Is order part of disorder, as we know it?

DB: What we mean by disorder is another question. It is not possible to give a coherent definition of disorder, because it violates order. Anything that actually happens has an order, but you can call a certain thing disorder if you like.

K: Are you saying that anything that happens is order?

DB: Has an order. If the body is not functioning rightly, even if cancer is growing, there is a certain order in the cancer cell; it is just growing according to a different pattern, which tends to break down the body. Nevertheless the whole thing has a certain kind of order.

K: Yes, yes.

DB: It has not violated the laws of nature, although relative to some context you could say it is disorder, because, if we are talking of the health of the body, then the cancer is called disorder. But in itself . . .

K: Cancer has its own order.

DB: Yes, but it is not compatible with the order of the growth of the body.

K: Quite. So what do we mean by order? Is there such a thing as order?

DB: Order is a perception; we can't get hold of order.

N: I think that generally when we refer to order it is in relation to a framework, or in relation to a certain field. Order always has that connotation. But when you say the order of order, as in the study of mathematics, we are going away from this limited approach to it.

DB: You see most mathematics start with the order of the numbers, like 1, 2, 3, 4, and build on that, in a hierarchy. But you can see what is meant by the order of the numbers. There is for example a series of relationships which are constant. In the order of the numbers, you have the simplest example of order.

N: And a new order was created with the discovery of zero! Are mathematical order and the order in nature, part of a bigger field? Or are these localized forms?

K: You see the brain, the mind, is so contradictory, so bruised, that it can't find order.

DB: Yes, but what kind of order does it want?

K: It wants an order in which it will be safe, in which it won't be bruised, be shocked, or feel physical and psychological pain.

DB: The whole point of order and mathematics is not to have contradiction.

K: But the brain is in contradiction.

DB: And something has gone wrong.

K: Yes, we have said that the brain took a wrong turn.

DB: You see, if the body is growing wrongly we have a cancer cell, which means two contradictory orders — one being the growth of the cancer, and the other the order of the body.

K: Yes. But can the mind, the brain, be totally free of all organized order?

DB: You mean by organized order, a fixed or imposed pattern?

K: Yes. Imposed or self-imposed. We are trying to investigate whether the brain can ever be free from all impositions, pressures, wounds, bruises and trivialities of existence which are pushing it in different directions. If it cannot, meditation has no meaning.

DB: You could go further, and say that probably life has no meaning if you cannot free it of all that.

K: No, I wouldn't say that life has no meaning.

DB: The pattern goes on indefinitely.

K: If it goes on as it has done, indefinitely, for millenia, life has no meaning. But I think there is a meaning and to find out, the brain must be totally free.

DB: What is the source of what we call disorder? It is like a cancer going on inside the brain, moving in a way which is not compatible with the health of the brain.

K: Yes.

DB: It grows as time goes on, it increases from one generation to another.

K: Each generation repeats the same pattern.

DB: It tends to accumulate through tradition with every generation.

K: How is this set, accumulated pattern, to end, to be broken through?

DB: Could we ask another question? Why does the brain provide the soil for this stuff to grow on?

K: It may be merely tradition or habit.

DB: But why does the brain stay in that?

K: It feels safe. It is afraid of something new taking place, because in the old tradition it finds refuge.

DB: Then we have to question why the brain deceives itself. This pattern involves the fact that the brain deceives itself about disorder. It doesn't seem able to see it clearly.

N: In my mind there is intelligence behind order which makes use of it. I have a certain purpose for which I create an order, and when the purpose is over I set aside that order or pattern. So order has an intelligence which works it out. That is the usual connotation. But you are referring to something else.

K: I am asking whether this pattern of generations can be broken, and why the brain has accepted that pattern in spite of all its conflicts and misery.

N: I am saying the same thing in a different way. When an order has served its purpose, can it then be put aside?

K: Apparently it can't. We are speaking pyschologically. It can't. The brain goes on, repeating fears, sorrow, miseries. Is it so heavily conditioned that it cannot see its way out of it, because, by constant repetition, the brain has become dull?

N: The momentum of repetition is there?

K: Yes. That momentum makes the mind mechanical. And in that sluggishness it takes refuge and says, 'It's all right, I can go on.' That's what most human beings do.

DB: That is part of the disorder. To think in that way is a manifestation of disorder.

K: Of course.

N: Do you connect order with intelligence? Or is order something that exists on its own?

DB: Intelligence involves order; it requires the perception of order in an orderly way, without contradiction. But I think that, in the terms of this discussion, we ourselves don't create this; we don't impose this order, but rather it is natural.

K: Yes. I am the ordinary man. I see that I am caught. My whole way of living and thinking is out of this enormous length of time. Time is my whole existence. In the past, which cannot be changed, I take refuge. Right?

DB: Well I think that if we were to talk to the so-called ordinary man, we would find he doesn't really understand that time is something that happens to him.

K: I am saying an ordinary man can see, after talking over with another, that his whole existence is based on time. And the mind takes refuge in time — in the past.

DB: What does that mean exactly? How does it take refuge?

K: Because the past cannot be changed.

DB: Yes, but people also think of the future. It is common to think that the future can change. The Communists have said, give up the past, we are going to change the future.

K: But we can't give up the past, even if we think we can.

DB: Then if even those who try not to take refuge in the past, can't give it up, it seems that whatever we do, we are stuck.

K: So the next step is, why does the brain accept this way of living? Why doesn't it break it down? Is it through laziness or that in breaking it down it has no hope?

DB: That is still the same question, of going from past to future.

K: Of course. So what is the brain to do? This is applicable to most people, isn't it?

DB: We haven't understood why, when people see that their behaviour is disorderly or irrational, they try to give up the past, but find they cannot.

K: Wait, Sir. If I give up the past, I have no existence. If I give up all my remembrances, I have nothing; I am nothing.

DB: I think some people like the Marxists would look at it a little differently. Marx said that it is necessary to transform the conditions of human society and that this will remove the past.

K: But it has not done so. It cannot be done.

DB: That is because when man tries to transform it he still works from the past.

K: Yes, that's what I am saying.

DB: If you say, don't depend on the past at all, then, as you have asked, what are we going to do?

K: I am nothing: is that the reason why we cannot possibly give up the past? Because my existence, my way of thinking, my life, *everything*, is from the past. And if you say, wipe that out, what have I left?

DB: I think you could say that obviously we have to keep certain things from the past, like useful knowledge.

K: Yes, we have been through all that.

DB: But you could ask, suppose we keep that useful part of the past, and wipe out all aspects of the past which are contradictory?

K: Which are all psychologically contradictory. Then what is left? Just going to the office? There is nothing. Is that the reason why we cannot give it up?

DB: There is still a contradiction in that, because if you say, 'what is left', you are still asking from the past.

K: Of course.

DB: Are you simply saying that when people talk of giving up the past, they are just not doing it, but merely turning this into another question which avoids the issue?

K: Because my whole being is the past; it has changed or been modified, but its roots are in the past.

DB: Now if you said, 'All right, give all that up and in the future you will have something quite different, and better', would people then be attracted to this?

K: But 'better' is still from the past.

DB: But people want to be assured of at least something.

K: That is just it. There is nothing. The ordinary human being wants something to which he can cling.

DB: He may feel, not that he is clinging to the past, but reaching for something.

K: If I reach something it is still the past.

DB: Yes, it has its roots in the past, but that is not often obvious, because people say it is a big, new revolutionary situation.

K: As long as I have my roots in the past there cannot be order.

DB: Because the past is pervaded with disorder.

K: Yes. And is my mind, my brain, willing to see that there is absolutely nothing if I give up the past?

DB: And nothing to reach for.

K: Nothing. There is no movement. Sometimes people dangle a carrot in front of me and, foolishly, I follow it. But I see that there are really no carrots, no rewards or punishments. Then how is this past to be dissolved? Because otherwise I am still living in the field of time that is man-made. So what shall I do? Am I willing to face absolute emptiness?

DB: What will you tell somebody who is not willing to face this?

K: I am not bothered. If somebody says that he can't do all this, I say, 'Well, carry on'.

But I am willing to let my past go completely. Which means there is no effort or reward; nothing. And the brain is willing to face this extraordinary and totally new state of existing in nothingness. That is appallingly frightening.

DB: Even these words will have their meaning rooted in the past.

K: Of course. We have understood that; the word is not the thing. The mind says it is willing to do that, to face this absolute emptiness, because it has seen for itself that all the places where it has taken refuge are illusions . . .

DB: I think this leaves out something that you brought up earlier — the question of the damage of scars to the brain.

K: That is just it.

DB: The brain that isn't damaged could possibly let go the past fairly readily.

K: Look, can I discover what has caused damage to the brain? Surely one of the factors is strong, sustained emotions, like hatred.

DB: Probably a flash of emotion doesn't do so much damage, but people sustain it.

K: Of course. Hatred, anger and violence not only shock but wound the brain. Right?

DB: And getting excessively excited.

K: Of course; and drugs, etc. The natural response doesn't damage the brain. Now the brain is damaged; suppose it has been damaged through anger?

DB: You could even say that nerves probably get connected up in the wrong way, and that the connections are too fixed. I think there is evidence that these things will actually change the structure.

K: Yes, and can we have an insight into the whole nature of disturbance, so that the insight changes the cells of the brain which have been wounded?

DB: Well, possibly it would start them healing.

K: All right. That healing must be immediate.

DB: It may take time in the sense that, if wrong connections have been made, it is going to take time to redistribute the material. The beginning of it, it seems to me, is immediate.

K: All right. Can I do that? I have listened to 'X', I have carefully read, I have thought about all this, and I see that anger, violence, hatred — any excessive emotion — bruises the brain. And insight into this whole business brings about a mutation in the cells. It is so. Also the nerves — the adjustments, will be as rapid as possible.

DB: Something happens with cancer cells. Sometimes the cancer suddenly stops growing, and it goes the other way, for some reason that is unknown. But a change must have taken place in those cells.

K: Could it be that the brain cells change fundamentally, and the cancer process stops?

DB: Yes. Fundamentally it stops, and begins to dismantle.

K: Dismantle, yes that is it.

N: You are saying that insight sets into motion the right kind of connections, and stops the wrong connections?

DB: And it even dismantles the wrong connections.

N: So a beginning is made, and it is made *now*.

DB: At one moment.

K: That is the insight.

N: But there is no time involved, because the right movement has started now.

There is another thing which I want to ask about the past: for most people, the past means pleasure.

K: Not only pleasure but the remembrance of everything.

N: One starts disliking pleasure only when it becomes stale, or leads to difficulties. One wants pleasure all the time.

K: Of course.

N: It is sometimes difficult to distinguish between pleasure and the staleness or the difficulties that it brings.

K: Pleasure is always the past; there is no pleasure at the moment it is happening. That comes in later, when it is remembered. So the remembrance is the past. But I am willing to face nothingness which means to wipe out all that!

N: But I am saying that the human being, even though he understands what you are saying, is held back in this field.

K: Because he is not willing to face this emptiness. Pleasure is not compassion. Pleasure is not love, pleasure has no place in compassion. But perhaps if there is this mutation, compassion is stronger than pleasure.

DB: Even the perception of order may be stronger than pleasure. If people are really concerned with something, the pleasure plays no role at that moment.

N: But what happens to a man in whom pleasure is dominant?

K: We have already discussed this. As long as he is unwilling to face this extraordinary emptiness, he will keep on with the old pattern.

DB: You see, we have to say that this man had a damaged brain too. It is brain damage which causes this emphasis on pleasure, as well as the fear and the anger.

K: But the damaged brain is healed when there is insight.

DB: Yes. But I think many people who would understand that hate and anger are products of the damaged brain would find it hard to see that pleasure also is the product of the damaged brain.

K: Oh, yes, but of course it is.

DB: Can we say there is a true enjoyment, which is not the product of the damaged brain, which is confused with pleasure . . . ?

N: If pleasure gives rise to anger, anger is part of the damaged brain.

K: And also the demand for pleasure.

So do you have an insight into how very destructive the past is to the brain? Can the brain itself see, have an insight into this, and move out of it?

N: You are saying that the beginning of order comes from insight?

K: Obviously. Let's work from there.

N: May I put it in a different way? Is it possible to gather a certain amount of order in a pattern sense, artificially, so that it gives rise to a certain amount of insight?

K: Ah! You cannot find truth through the false.

N: I am asking it purposefully because many people seem to lack the energy that is required for insight.

K: You are tremendously keen to earn a livelihood, to earn money, to do anything in which you are really interested. If you are interested vitally in this transformation, etc., you have the energy.

May we go on? I, as a human being, have seen that this insight has wiped away the past, and the brain is willing to live in nothingness. Right? We have come to this point several times from different directions. Now let's go on. Now there isn't a thing put there by thought. There is no movement of thought, except factual knowledge which has its own place. But talking psychologically, there is no movement in the mind or of thought. There is absolutely nothing.

DB: You mean no feeling either? You see, the movement of thought and feeling is together.

K: Wait a minute. What do you mean here by feeling?

DB: Well, usually people might say, all right, there is no thought, but they have various feelings.

K: Of course we have feelings.

DB: These are sensations. And also there are the inner feelings.

K: Inner feelings of what?

DB: It is hard to describe them. Those that can easily be described are obviously the wrong kind, such as anger and fear.

K: Is compassion a feeling?

DB: Probably not.

K: No, it is not a feeling.

DB: Though people may say they *feel* compassionate! Even the very word suggests it is a form of feeling. Compassion has in it the word 'passion', which is feeling. This is a difficult question. We could perhaps question what we usually recognize as feelings?

K: Let's go into that a little bit. What do we mean by feelings? Sensations?

DB: Well, people don't usually mean that. You see, sensations are connected with the body.

K: So you are talking of feelings which are not of the body?

DB: Yes, or which — in the old days — would have been described as of the soul.

K: The soul, of course. That is an easy escape but it means nothing.

DB: No.

K: What are the inner feelings? Pleasure?

DB: Well, in so far as you could label it, that description would not be valid.

K: So what is valid? The non-verbal state?

DB: It may be a non-verbal state . . . something analogous to a feeling which isn't fixed, that can't be named.

N: You are saying it is not feeling, it is similar to feeling, but it is not fixed?

DB: Yes. I am just considering that that could exist if we say that there is no thought. I am trying to clarify this.

K: Yes, there is no thought.

DB: What does that really mean?

K: What it really means is, thought is movement, thought is time. Right? In that emptiness there is not time or thought.

DB: Yes, and perhaps no sense of the existence of an entity inside.

K: Absolutely, of course. The existence of the entity is the bundle of memories, the past.

DB: But that existence is not only thought thinking about it, but also the feeling that it is there; you get a sort of feeling inside.

K: A feeling, yes. There is no being. There is nothing. If there is a feeling of the being continuing . . .

DB: Yes, even though it doesn't seem possible to verbalize this . . . It would be a state without desire. How can we know if this state is real, is genuine?

K: That is what I am asking. How do we know, or realize that this is so? In other words, do you want proof of it?

N: Not proof, but communication of that state.

K: Now wait a minute. Suppose someone has this peculiar compassion, how can he communicate it to me, if I am living in pleasure and all that? He can't!

N: No, but I am prepared to listen to him.

K: Prepared to listen, but how deeply? The man says there is no being. And one's whole life has been this becoming. And, in that state, he says there is no being at all. In other words, there is no 'me'. Right? Now you say, 'Show it to me'. It can be shown only through certain qualities that it has, certain actions. What are the actions of a mind that is totally empty of being? Actions at what level? Actions in the physical world?

N: Partly.

K: Mostly that. All right, this man has got this sense of emptiness, and there is no being. He is not acting from self-centred interests. His actions are in the world of daily living, and you can judge whether he is a hypocrite, whether he says something and contradicts it the next moment, or whether he is actually living this compassion and not just saying, 'I feel compassionate'.

DB: But if one is not doing the same, one can't tell.

K: That's right. That is what I am saying.

N: We can't judge him.

K: You can't. So how can he convey to us in words that peculiar quality of mind? He can describe, go round it, but he can't give the essence of it. Dr. Bohm, for example, could discuss with Einstein; they were on the same level. And he and I can discuss. If one has this sense of not being, of emptiness, the other can go very close, but can never enter that mind unless he has it!

N: Is there any way of communicating, for one who is open, but not through words?

K: We are talking of compassion. It is not, 'I feel compassionate'. That is altogether wrong. You see, in daily life such a mind acts without the 'me', without the 'ego'. Therefore it might make a mistake, but it corrects immediately; it is not carrying that mistake.

N: It is not stuck.

K: Not stuck. But we must be very careful here not to find an excuse for wrong!
    So we come to that point that we discussed earlier; what then is meditation? Right? For the man who is becoming, meditation has no meaning whatsoever. That is a tremendous statement. When there is not this being or becoming, what is meditation? It must be totally unconscious, totally uninvited.

DB: Do you mean, without conscious intention?

K: Yes, I think that is right. Would you say — I hope this doesn't sound silly — that the universe, the cosmic order, is in meditation?

DB: Well, if it is alive, then we would have to look at it that way.

K: No, no. It is in a state of meditation.

DB: Yes.

K: I think that is right. I stick to that.

DB: We should try to go further into what is meditation. What is it doing?

N: If you say that the universe is in meditation, is the expression of it order? What order can we discern which would indicate cosmic or universal meditation?

K: The sunrise and sunset; all the stars, the planets are order. The whole thing is in perfect order.

DB: We have to connect this with meditation. According to the dictionary, the meaning of meditation is to reflect, to turn something over in the mind, and to pay close attention.

K: And also to measure.

DB: That is a further meaning, but it is to weigh, to ponder, it means 'measure' in the sense of weighing.

K: Weighing, that's it. Ponder, think over, and so on.

DB: To weigh the significance of something. Now is that what you mean?

K: No.

DB: Then why do you use the word?

N: I am told that, in English, contemplation has a different connotation from meditation. Contemplation implies a deeper state of mind.

DB: It is hard to know. The word 'contemplate' comes from the word temple, really.

K: Yes, that's right.

DB: Its basic meaning is, to create an open space.

K: Is that an open space between God and me?

DB: That is the way the word arose.

K: Quite.

N: The Sanskrit word Dhyans doesn't have the same connotation as meditation.

K: No.

N: Because meditation has the overtones of measurement, and probably, in an oblique way, that measurement is order.

K: No, I don't want to bring in order — let's leave the word order out. We have been through that, and beaten it to death!

DB: Why do you use the word meditation?

K: Don't let's use it.

DB: Let's find out what you really mean here.

K: Would you say, a state of infinity? A measureless state?

DB: Yes.

K: There is no division of any kind. You see we are giving lots of descriptions, but it is not that.

DB: Yes, but is there any sense of the mind being in some way aware of itself?
  Is that what you are trying to say? At other times you have said that the mind is emptying itself of content.

K: What are you trying to get at?

DB: I am asking whether it is not only infinite, but if something more is involved?

K: Oh, much more.

DB: We said that content is the past which is making disorder. Then you could say that this emptying of content in some sense is constantly cleaning up the past. Would you agree to that?

K: No, no.

DB: When you say the mind is emptying itself of content . . .

K: *Has* emptied itself.

DB: All right, then. When the past is cleaned up, then you say that is meditation.

K: That is meditation; no, contemplation . . .

N: Just a beginning.

K: Beginning?

N: The emptying of the past.

K:　That emptying of the past, which is anger, jealousy, beliefs, dogmas, attachments, etc., must be done. If that is not emptied, if any part of that exists, it will inevitably lead to illusion. The brain or the mind must be totally free of all illusion, illusion brought by desire, by hope, by wanting security, and all that.

DB:　Are you saying that when this is done, it opens the door to something broader, deeper?

K:　Yes. Otherwise life has no meaning; it is just repeating this pattern.

N:　What exactly did you mean when you said that the universe is in meditation?

K:　I feel that way, yes.

DB:　Could we say first of all that the universe is not actually governed by its past? You see, the universe creates certain forms which are relatively constant, so that people who look at it superficially only see that, and it seems then to be determined from the past.

K:　Yes, it is not governed by the past. It is creative, moving.

DB:　And then this movement is order.

K:　Would you, as a scientist, accept such a thing?

DB:　Well as a matter of fact I would!

K:　Are we both crazy? Let's put the question another way: is it really possible for time to end — the whole idea of time as the past — chronologically, so that there is no tomorrow at all? There is the feeling, the actual reality, psychologically, of having no tomorrow. I think that is the healthiest way of living — which doesn't mean that I become irresponsible! That would be too childish.

DB:　It is merely a question of physical time, which is a certain part of natural order.

K:　Of course; that is understood.

DB:　The question is whether we have a sense of experiencing past and future or whether we are free of that sense.

K:　I am asking you, as a scientist, is the universe based on time?

DB: I would say no, but you see the general way . . .

K: That is all I want. You say no! And can the brain, which has evolved in time . . . ?

DB: Well, has it evolved in time? Rather it has become entangled in time. Because the brain is part of the universe, which we say is not based on time.

K: I agree.

DB: Thought has entangled the brain in time.

K: All right. Can that entanglement be unravelled, freed, so that the universe is the mind? You follow? If the universe is not of time, can the mind, which has been entangled in time, unravel itself and so be the universe? You follow what I am trying to say?

DB: Yes.

K: That is order.

DB: That is order. And would you say that it is meditation?

K: That is it. I would call that meditation, not in the ordinary, dictionary sense of pondering, and all that, but a state of meditation in which there is no element of the past.

DB: You say the mind is disentangling itself from time, and also really disentangling the brain from time?

K: Yes, would you accept that?

DB: Yes.

K: As a theory?

DB: Yes, as a proposal.

K: No, I don't want it as a proposal.

DB: What do you mean by theory?

K: Theory — when somebody comes along and says, this is real meditation.

DB: All right.

K: Wait. Somebody says, one can live this way; life has an extraordinary meaning in it, full of compassion, etc., and every act in the physical world can be corrected immediately, and so on. Would you, as a scientist, accept such a state, or say that the man who talks of it is cuckoo?

DB: No, I wouldn't say that. I feel it is perfectly possible; it is quite compatible with anything that I know about nature.

K: Oh, then that's all right. So one is not an unbalanced cuckoo! Of course putting all this into words is not the thing. Right? That is understood. But can it be communicated to another? Now can some of us get to this, so that we can communicate it, actually?

7 JUNE 1980, BROCKWOOD PARK, HAMPSHIRE

ELEVEN

The Ending of 'Psychological' Knowledge

KRISHNAMURTI: What makes the mind always follow a certain pattern? Always seeking? If it lets go of one pattern it picks up another; it keeps on functioning all the time like that. One can give explanations of why it does so — for protection, for safety, from indifference, a certain amount of callousness, a disregard of one's own flowering, etc.

But it is really very important to explore deeply why our minds are always operating in a certain direction.

We said that one comes, after going through travail, investigation, and insight, to a blank wall. And that blank wall can only wither away, or be broken down, when there is love and intelligence. Before we go into that, I would like to ask why human beings, however intelligent, however learned, however philosophical and religious, always fall into this groove of pattern seeking.

DAVID BOHM: Well, I think the groove is inherent in the nature of the accumulated knowledge.

K: Are you saying then that knowledge must invariably create a groove?

DB: Perhaps it is not inevitable but it seems to develop this way in mankind, if we are referring to psychological knowledge, that is to say . . .

K: Obviously we are talking of that. But why does the mind not become aware of it — see the danger of this mechanical repetition, and the fact that there is nothing new in it? See how we keep on doing it?

DB: It seems to me that the groove, or the accumulated knowledge, seems to have a significance far beyond what its significance is. If we say that we have knowledge of some object, like the microphone, that has some limited significance. But knowledge about the nation to which you belong seems to have immense significance.

K: Yes. So is this attribution of significance the cause of the narrowing down of the mind?

DB: Because this knowledge seems to have a tremendous value beyond all other values, it makes the mind stick to that. It seems the most important thing in the world.

K: In India, there is this philosophy that knowledge must end — you know it, of course, the Vedanta. But apparently very, very, few people do end knowledge and talk from freedom.

DB: You see, knowledge generally seems to be extremely important, even when a person may say verbally that it should end . . .

K: You mean I am so stupid that I don't see that this psychological knowledge has very little significance, and so my mind clings to it?

DB: I wouldn't quite put it that a person is that stupid, but rather say that his knowledge stupefies the brain.

K: Stupefied, all right. But the brain doesn't seem to extricate itself.

DB: It is already so stupefied that it can't see what it is doing.

K: So what shall it do? I have been watching for many years people attempting to become free from certain things. This is the root of it, you understand? This psychological accumulation which becomes psychological knowledge. And so it divides, and all kinds of things happen around it and within it. And yet the mind refuses to let go.

DB: Yes.

K: Why? Is that because there is safety or security in it?

DB: That is part of it, but I think in some way that knowledge has taken on the significance of the absolute, instead of being relative.

K: I understand all that, but you are not answering my question. I am an ordinary man, I realize all this, and the limited significance of knowledge at different levels, but deeper down inside one, this accumulated knowledge is very destructive.

DB: The knowledge deceives the mind, so that the person is not normally aware that it is destructive. Once this process gets started, the mind is not in a state where it is able to look at it because it is avoiding the question. There is a tremendous defensive mechanism or escape from looking at the whole issue.

K: Why?

DB: Because it seems that something extremely precious might be at stake.

K: One is strangely intelligent, capable or skilled in other directions, but here, where the root is of all this trouble, why don't we comprehend what is happening? What prevents the mind from doing this?

DB: Once importance has been given to knowledge, there is a mechanical process that resists intelligence.

K: So what shall I do? I realize I must let go the accumulated, psychological knowledge — which is divisive, destructive and petty — but I can't. Is this because of lack of energy?

DB: Not primarily, though the energy is being dissipated by the process.

K: Having dissipated a great deal of energy, I haven't the energy to grapple with this?

DB: The energy would come back quickly if we could under-stand this. I don't think that is the main point.

K: No. So what shall I do, realizing that this knowledge is inevitably forming a groove in which I live? How am I to break it down?

DB: Well, I am not sure that it is generally clear to people that this knowledge does all that; or that the knowledge *is* knowledge. You see, it may seem to be some 'being', the 'self', and 'me'. This knowledge creates the 'me', and the 'me' is the experience as an entity, which seems not to be knowledge but some real being.

K: Are you saying that this 'being' is different from knowledge?

DB: It appears to be; it feigns a difference.

K: But is it?

DB: It isn't, but the illusion has great power.

K: That has been our conditioning.

DB: Yes. Now the question is, how do we get through that to break down the groove, because it creates the imitation, or a pretension, of a state of being?

K: That is the real point, you see. This is man's central movement. It seems so utterly hopeless. And realizing the hopelessness I sit down and say I can't do anything. But if I apply my mind to it, the question arises, is it possible to function without psychological knowledge in this world? I am rather concerned about it; it seems the basic issue that man must resolve, all over the world.

DB: That is right. But you may discuss with somebody, who thinks it seems reasonable. But perhaps his status is threatened, and we have to say that that is psychological knowledge. It doesn't seem to him that it is knowledge, but something more. And he doesn't see that his knowledge of his status is behind the trouble. At first sight knowledge *seems* to be something passive, which you could use if you wanted to, and which you could just put aside if you wished, which is the way it should be.

K: I understand all that.

DB: But then the moment comes when knowledge no longer appears to be knowledge.

K: The politicians and the people in power wouldn't listen to this. And neither would the so-called religious people. It is only the people who are discontented, who feel they have lost everything, who will listen. But they don't always listen so that it is a real burning thing.

How does one go about this? Say, for instance, I have left Catholicism and Protestantism, and all that. Also I have a career and I know that it is necessary to have knowledge there. Now I see how important it is not to be caught in the process of psychological knowledge, and yet I can't let it go. It is always dodging me; I am playing tricks with it. It is like hide and seek. All right! We said that is the wall I have to break down. No, not I — that is the wall that has to be broken down. And we have said that this wall can be

broken down through love and intelligence. Aren't we asking
something enormously difficult?

DB: It is difficult.

K: I am this side of the wall, and you are asking me to have that
love and intelligence which will destroy it. But I don't know what
that love is, what that intelligence is, because I am caught in this,
on this other side of the wall. I realize logically, sanely, that what
you are saying is accurate, true, logical, and I see the importance
of it, but the wall is so strong and dominant and powerful that I
can't get beyond it. We said the other day that the wall could be
broken down through insight — if insight does not become
translated into an idea.

DB: Yes.

K: When insight is discussed, there is the danger of our making
an abstraction of it; which means we move away from the fact, and
the abstraction becomes all important. Which means, again,
knowledge.

DB: Yes, the activity of knowledge.

K: So we are back again!

DB: I think the general difficulty is that knowledge is not just
sitting there as a form of information, but is extremely active,
meeting and shaping every moment according to past knowledge.
So even when we raise this issue, knowledge is all the time waiting,
and then acting. Our whole tradition is that knowledge is not
active but passive. But it is really active, although people don't
generally think of it that way. They think it is just sitting there.

K: It is waiting.

DB: Waiting to act, you see. And whatever we try to do about it,
knowledge is already acting. By the time we realize that this is the
problem, it has already acted.

K: Yes. But do I realize it as a problem, or as an idea which I
must carry out? You see the difference?

DB: Knowledge automatically turns everything into an idea,
which we must carry out. That is the whole way it is built.

K: The whole way we have lived.

DB: Knowledge can't do anything else.

K: How are we to break that, even for a second?

DB: It seems to me that if you could see, observe, be aware — if knowledge could be aware of itself at work . . . The point is that knowledge seems to work unawares, simply waiting, and then acting, by which time it has disrupted the order of the brain.

K: I am very concerned about this because wherever I go this is what is happening. It is something that has to be resolved. Would you say the capacity to listen is far more important than any of this, than any explanations, or logic?

DB: It comes to the same problem.

K: No, no. It doesn't. I want to see if there is a possibility that when I listen completely to what you are saying, the wall has broken down. You understand? Is there — I am trying to find out, Sir — I am an ordinary man and you are telling me all this, and I realize what you are saying is so. I am really deeply involved in what you are saying, but somehow the flame isn't lit; all the fuel is there, but the fire is not. So what shall I do? This is my everlasting cry!

DB: The brain has the capacity to listen; we have to question whether the ordinary man is so full of opinions that he can't listen.

K: You can't listen with opinions; you might just as well be dead.

DB: I think knowledge has all sorts of defences. Is it possible for, say, the ordinary man to have this perception? That is really what you are asking, isn't it?

K: Yes. But there must be a communication between you and that man, something so strong that the very act of his listening to you, and you communicating with him, operates.

DB: Yes, then you have to break through his opinions, through the whole structure.

K: Of course. That is why this man has come here — for that. He has finished with all the churches and doctrines. He realizes that what has been said here is true. When you communicate with him, your communication is strong and real, because you are not speaking from knowledge or opinions. A free human being is trying to communicate with this ordinary man. Now can he listen with that intensity which you, the communicator, are giving him? He wants to listen to somebody who is telling the truth, and in the very telling of it, something is taking place in him. Because he is so ardently listening, this happens.

It is rather like you as a scientist, telling one of your students something. You are telling him about something which must be enormously important, because you have given your life to it. And the student has given up much just to come here. Is it the fault of the communicator that the listener does not receive it instantly? Or is the listener incapable of hearing it?

DB: Well, if he is incapable of listening, then nothing can be done. But let's say there is somebody who comes along who has got through some of these defences, although there are others that he is not aware of — that is something less simple than what you have described.

K: I feel it is dreadfully simple somehow. If one could listen with all one's being, the brain would not be caught in the groove. You see, generally, in communication, you are telling me something and I am absorbing it, but there is an interval between you telling and my absorbing.

DB: Yes.

K: And that interval is the danger. If I don't absolutely absorb, listen with all my being, it is finished. Is listening difficult because in this there is no shadow of pleasure? You are not offering any pleasure, any gratification. You are saying this is so; take it. But my mind is so involved in pleasure that it won't listen to anything that is not completely satisfactory or pleasurable.

I realize too the danger of that. Of seeking satisfaction and pleasure, so I put that aside too. There is no pleasure, no reward, no punishment. In listening, there is only pure observation.

So we come to the point, is pure observation, which is actually listening, love? I think it is.

Again, if you state this, then my mind says 'Give it to me. Tell me what to do.' But when I ask you to tell me what to do, I am back in the field of knowledge. It is so instantaneous. So I refuse to ask you what to do. Then where am I? You have referred to perception without any motive or direction. Pure perception is love. And in that perception love is intelligence. They are not three separate things, they are all one thing. You pointed all this out very carefully, step by step, and I have come to that point that I have a feeling for it. But it goes away so quickly. Then the question begins, 'How am I to get it back?' Again, the remembrance of it, which is knowledge, blocks.

DB: What you are saying is that every time there is a communication, knowledge begins to work in many different forms.

K: So you see it is enormously difficult to be free of knowledge.

DB: We could ask, why doesn't knowledge wait until it is needed?

K: That means to be psychologically free of knowledge, but, when the need arises, to act from freedom, not from knowledge.

DB: But knowledge comes in to inform your action, although it is not the source.

K: That is freedom from knowledge. And being free, it is from freedom and not from knowledge that one communicates. That is, from emptiness there is communication. When we use words, they are the outcome of knowledge, but they are from that state of complete freedom. Now, suppose I, as an ordinary human being, have come to that point where there is this freedom, and from it communication takes place — will you, as an eminent scientist, communicate with me without any barrier? You follow what I am saying?

DB: Yes. There is this freedom from knowledge when knowledge is seen to be information. But ordinarily it seems more than information, and knowledge itself does not see that knowledge is not free.

K: It is never free. And if I am going to understand myself, I must be free to look.
   How will you communicate with me, who have come to a certain point where I am burning to receive what you are saying, so completely that psychological knowledge is finished? Or am I fooling myself about being in that state?

DB: Well, that is the question: knowledge is constantly deceiving itself.

K: So is my mind always deceiving itself? Then what shall I do? Let's come back to that.

DB: Again I think the answer is to listen.

K: Why don't we listen? Why don't we *immediately* understand this thing? One can give all the superficial reasons why — old age, conditioning, laziness, and so on.

DB: But is it possible to give the deep reason for it?

K: I think it is that the knowledge which is the 'me' is so tremendously strong as an idea.

DB: Yes, that is why I tried to say that the idea has tremendous significance and meaning. For example, suppose you have the idea of God; this takes on a tremendous power.

K: Or if I have the idea that I am British, or French, it gives me great energy.

DB: And so it creates a state of the body which seems the very being of the self. Now the person doesn't experience it as mere knowledge . . .

K: Yes, but are we going round and round and round? It seems like it.

DB: Well, I was wondering if there is anything that could be communicated about that overwhelming power that seems to come with knowledge . . .

K: . . . and with identification.

DB: That seems to be something that would be worth looking into.

K: Now what is the root meaning of 'identification'?

DB: Always the same.

K: Always the same, that's right. That's right! There is nothing new under the sun.

DB: You say the self is always the same. It tries to be always the same in essence, if not in detail.

K: Yes, yes.

DB: I think this is the thing that goes wrong with knowledge. It attempts to be involved with what is always the same, so it sticks, you see. Knowledge itself tries to find what is permanent and perfect. I mean, even independent of any of us. It is like building it into the cells.

K: From this arises the question, is it possible to attend diligently? I am using 'diligence' in the sense of being accurate.

DB: Actually it means to take pains.

K: Of course. To take pains, take the whole of it. There must be some other way round all this intellectual business. We have exercised a great deal of it and that intellectual capacity has led to the blank wall. I approach it from every direction, but eventually the wall is there, which is the 'me', with my knowledge, my prejudice, and all the rest of it. And the 'me' then says, 'I must do something about it.' Which is still the 'me'.

DB: The 'me' wants always to be constant, but at the same time it tries to change.

K: To put on a different coat. It is always the same. So the mind which is functioning with the 'me' is always the same mind. Good Lord, you see, we are back again!

We have tried everything — fasting, every kind of discipline — to get rid of the 'me' with all its knowledge and illusions. One tries to identify with something else, which is the same thing. One then comes back to the fundamental question, what will make the blank wall totally disappear? I think this is only possible when the man who is blocked can give total attention to what the free man is saying. There is no other means to break down the wall — not the intellect, not the emotions, nor anything else. When somebody who has gone beyond the wall, who has broken it down, says, 'Listen, for God's sake listen,' and I listen to him with my mind empty, then it is finished. You know what I am saying? I have no sense of hoping for anything to happen, or anything to come back, or concern with the future. The mind is empty, and therefore listening. It is finished.

For a scientist to discover something new, he must have a certain emptiness from which there will be a different perception.

DB: Yes, but only in the sense that usually the question is limited, and so the mind may be empty with regard to that particular question, allowing the discovery of an insight in that area. But we are not questioning this particular area. We are questioning the whole of knowledge.

K: It is most extraordinary when you go into it.

DB: And you were saying the end of knowledge is the Vedanta.

K: That is the real answer.

DB: But generally people feel they must keep knowledge in one area to be able to question it in another. You see it might worry people to ask, with what knowledge do I question the whole of knowledge?

K: Yes. With what knowledge do I question my knowledge? Quite.

DB: In a way, we do have knowledge, because we have seen that this whole structure of psychological knowledge makes no sense, that it is inconsistent and has no meaning.

K: From that emptiness that we were talking of, is there a ground or a source from which all things begin? Matter, human beings, their capacities, their idiocies — does the whole movement start from there?

DB: We could consider that. But let's try to clarify it a little. We have the emptiness.

K: Yes, emptiness in which there is no movement of thought as psychological knowledge. And therefore no psychological time.

DB: Though we still have the time of the watch . . .

K: Yes, but we have gone beyond that; don't let's go back to it. There is no psychological time, no movement of thought. And is that emptiness the beginning of all movement?

DB: Well, would you say the emptiness is the ground?

K: That is what I am asking. Let's go slowly into this.

DB: Earlier on, we were saying that there is the emptiness, and beyond that is the ground.

K: I know, I know. Let's discuss this further.

18 SEPTEMBER 1980, BROCKWOOD PARK, HAMPSHIRE

TWELVE

The Mind in the Universe

KRISHNAMURTI: We talked the other day about a mind that is entirely free from all movement, from all the things that thought has put there, the past, and the future, and so on. But before we go into that I would like to discuss man's being caught in materialistic attitudes and values, and to ask, what is the nature of materialism?

DAVID BOHM: Well, first of all materialism is the name of a certain philosophical . . .

K: I don't mean that. I want to explore this.

DB: Matter is all there is, you see.

K: That is, nature and all human beings, react physically. This reaction is sustained by thought. And thought is a material process. So reaction in nature is a materialistic response.

DB: I think the word 'materialistic' is not quite right. It is the response of matter.

K: The response of matter; let's put it that way. That is better. We are talking about having an empty mind, and we have come to that point when the wall has been broken down. This emptiness and what lies beyond it, or through it — we will come to that, but before doing so, I am asking, is all reaction matter?

DB: Matter in movement. You could say that there is evidence in favour of that, that science has found a tremendous number of reactions which are due to the nerves.

K: So would you say that matter and movement are the reactions which exist in all organic matter?

DB: Yes, all matter as we know it goes by the law of action and reaction, you see. Every action has a corresponding reaction.

K: So action and reaction are a material process, as is thought. Now, to go beyond it is the issue.

DB: But before we say that, some people might feel that there is no meaning in going beyond it. That would be the philosophy of materialism.

K: But if one is merely living in that area it is very, very shallow. Right? It has really no meaning at all.

DB: Perhaps one should refer to one thing that people have said — that matter is not merely action and reaction, but may have a creative movement. You see, matter may create new forms.

K: But it is still in that area.

DB: Yes. Let's try to make it clear. We have to see that there are very subtle forms of materialism which might be difficult to pin down.

K: Let's begin. Would you consider that thought is a material process?

DB: Yes. Well, some people might argue that it is both material, and something beyond material.

K: I know. I have discussed this. But it is not.

DB: How can we say that simply, to make it clear?

K: Because any movement of thought is a material process.

DB: Well, we have to amplify this so that it is not a matter of authority. As an observation, one sees that thought is a material process. Now how are you going to see that?

K: How could one be aware that thought is a material process? I think that is fairly clear. There is an experience, an incident which is recorded, which becomes knowledge. And from that knowledge, thought arises and action takes place.

DB: Yes. So we say that thought is that. It is still coming from the background. So are you saying that something new coming into being is not part of this process?

K: Yes, if there is to be something new, thought, as a material process, must end. Obviously.

DB: And then it may take it up later.

K: Later, yes. Wait, see what happens later. So we say all action, reaction and action from that reaction is movement of matter.

DB: Yes, very subtle movement of matter.

K: So as long as one's mind is within that area, it must be a movement of matter. So is it possible for the mind to go beyond reaction? That is the next step. As we said earlier one gets irritated, and that is the first reaction. Then the reaction to that, the second reaction, is 'I must not be'. Then the third reaction is, 'I must control or justify'. So it is constantly action and reaction. Can one see that this is a continuous movement without an ending?

DB: Yes. The reaction is continuous, but it seems at a certain moment to have ended, and the next moment appears to be a new movement.

K: But it is still reaction.

DB: It is still the same but it presents itself differently.

K: It is exactly the same always . . .

DB: But it presents itself as always different, always new.

K: Of course. That's just it. You say something, I get irritated, but that irritation is a reaction.

DB: Yes, it *seems* to be something suddenly new.

K: But it is not.

DB: But one has to be aware of that, you see. Generally the mind tends not to be aware of it.

K: We are sensitive to it, alert to the question. So there is an ending to reaction if one is watchful, attentive; if one understands not only logically, but having an insight into this reacting process, it can of course come to an end. That is why it is very important to understand this, before we discuss what is an empty mind, and if there is something beyond this, or whether in that very emptying of the mind there is some other quality.

So is that empty mind a reaction? A reaction to the problems of pain and pleasure and suffering? An attempt to escape from all this into some state of nothingness?

DB: Yes, the mind can always do that.

K: It can invent. Now we have come to the point of asking whether this quality of emptiness is not a reaction. Right, Sir? Before we go further, is it possible to have a mind that is really *completely* empty of all the things that thought has put together?

DB: So that thought ceases to act.

K: That's it.

DB: On the one hand, perhaps you could say that reaction is due to the nature of matter, which is continually reacting and moving. But then is matter affected by this insight?

K: I don't quite follow. Ah, I understand! Does insight affect the cells of the brain which contain the memory?

DB: Yes. The memory is continually reacting, moving, as does the air and the water, and everything around us.

K: After all, if I don't react physically I am paralysed. But to be reacting continuously is also a form of paralysis.

DB: Well, the wrong kind of reaction! Reaction around the psychological structure. But assuming that the reaction around the psychological structure has begun in mankind, why should it ever stop? Because reaction makes another and another, and one would expect it to go on for ever, and that nothing would stop it.

K: Only insight into the nature of reaction ends psychological reaction.

DB: Then you are saying that matter is affected by insight which is beyond matter.

K: Yes, beyond matter. So is this emptiness within the brain itself? Or is it something that thought has conceived as being empty? One must be very clear.

DB: Yes. But whatever we discuss, no matter what the question is, thought begins to want to do something about it, because thought feels it can always make a contribution.

K: Quite.

DB: Thought in the past did not understand that it has no useful contribution to make, but it has kept on in the habit of trying to say that emptiness is very good. Therefore thought says, I will try to bring about the emptiness.

K: Of course.

DB: Thought is trying to be helpful!

K: We have been through all that. We have seen the nature of thought, and its movement, time, and all that. But I want to find out whether this emptiness is within the mind itself, or beyond it.

DB: What do you mean by the mind?

K: The mind is the whole — emotions, thought, consciousness, the brain — the whole of that is the mind.

DB: The word 'mind' has been used in many ways. Now you are using it in a certain way, that it represents thought, feeling, desire and will — the whole material process.

K: Yes, the whole material process.

DB: Which people have called non-material!

K: Quite. But the mind is the whole material process.

DB: Which is going on in the brain and the nerves.

K: The whole structure. One can see that this materialistic reaction can end. And the next question I am asking is whether that emptiness is within or without. (Without, in the sense of being elsewhere.)

DB: Where would it be?

K: I don't think it *would* be elsewhere, but I am just putting the question . . .

DB: Well, any such thing is a material process.

K: It is in the mind itself. Not outside it. Right?

DB: Yes.

K: Now what is the next step? Does that emptiness contain nothing? Not a thing?

DB: Not a thing, by which we mean anything that has form, structure, stability.

K: Yes. All that, form, structure, reaction, stability, capacity. Then what is it? Is it then total energy?

DB: Yes, movement of energy.

K: Movement of energy. It is not movement of reaction.

DB: It is not movement of things reacting to each other. The world can be regarded as made up of a number of things which react to each other and that is one kind of movement: but we are saying it is a different kind of movement.

K: Entirely different.

DB: There is no thing in it.

K: No thing in it, and therefore it is not of time. Is that possible? Or are we just indulging in imagination? In some kind of romantic, hopeful, pleasurable sensation? I don't think that we are, because we have been through all that, step by step, right up to this point. So we are not deceiving ourselves. Now we say that emptiness has no centre, as the 'me', and all the reactions. In that emptiness there is a movement of timeless energy.

DB: When you refer to timeless energy, we could repeat what we have already said about time and thought being the same.

K: Yes, of course.

DB: Then you were saying that time can only come into a material process?

K: That's right.

DB: Now if we have energy that is timeless but nevertheless moving . . .

K: Yes, not static . . .

DB: Then what is the movement?

K: What is movement from here to here?

DB: That is one form.

K: One form. Or from yesterday to today, and from today to tomorrow.

DB: There are various kinds of movement.

K: So what is movement? Is there a movement which is not a movement? You understand? Is there a movement which has no beginning and no end? Unlike thought which has a beginning and an end.

DB: Except you could say that the movement of matter might have a beginning and no ending; the reactive movement. You are not speaking of that?

K: No, I am not talking of that. Thought has a beginning and thought has an ending. There is a movement of matter as reaction, and the ending of that reaction.

DB: In the brain.

K: Yes. But there are various kinds of movements. That is all we know. And someone comes along and says there is a totally different kind of movement. But to understand that, we must be free of the movement of thought, and the movement of time, to understand a movement that is not . . .

DB: Well there are two things about this movement. It has no beginning and no end, but also it is not determined as a series of successions from the past.

K: Of course. No causation.

DB: But you see, matter can be looked at as a series of causes; it may not be adequate. But now you are saying that this movement has no beginning and no ending; it is not the result of a series of causes following one another.

K: So I want to understand verbally a movement that is not a movement. I don't know if I am making it clear?

DB: Then why is it called a movement if it is not a movement?

K: Because it is not still, it is active.

DB: It is energy.

K: It has tremendous energy; therefore it can never be still. But in that energy it has stillness.

DB: I think we have to say that the ordinary language does not convey this properly, but the energy itself is still, and also moving.

K: But in that movement is a movement of stillness. Does it sound crazy?

DB: The movement can be said to emerge from stillness.

K: That's right. You see, that is what it is. We said that this emptiness is in the mind. It has no cause and no effect. It is not a movement of thought, of time. It is not a movement of material reactions. None of that. Which means, is the mind capable of that extraordinary stillness without any movement? When it is so completely still, there is a movement out of it.

DB: I think I mentioned before that some people, like Aristotle, had this notion in the past; we discussed it. He talked about the unmoved mover, when trying to describe God, you see.

K: Ah, God, no. I don't want to do that!

DB: You don't want to describe God, but some sort of notion similar to this has been held in the past by various people. Since then it has gone out of fashion, I think.

K: Let's bring it into fashion, shall we?!

DB: I am not saying that Aristotle had the right idea. It is merely that he was considering something somewhat similar, though probably different in many respects.

K: Was it an intellectual concept or an actuality?

DB: This is very hard to tell because so little is known.

K: Therefore we don't have to bring in Aristotle.

DB: I merely wanted to point out that the concept of a movement of stillness wasn't crazy, because other very respectable people had had something similar.

K: I am glad! I am glad to be assured that I am not crazy!
And is that movement out of stillness the movement of creation? We are not talking of what the poets, writers and painters call creation. To me, that is not creation; just capacity, skill, memory and knowledge operating. Here I think this creation is not expressed in form.

DB: It is important to differentiate. Usually we think creation is expressed in form, or as structure.

K: Yes, structure. We have gone beyond being crazy, so we can go on! Would you say that this movement, not being of time, is eternally new?

DB: Yes. It is eternally new in the sense that the creation is eternally new. Right?

K: Creation is eternally new. You see that newness is what the artists are trying to discover. Therefore they indulge in all kinds of absurdities, but few come to that point where the mind is absolutely silent, and out of that silence there is this movement which is always new. The moment when that movement is expressed . . .

DB: . . . the first expression is in thought?

K: That is just it.

DB: And that may be useful, but then it gets fixed, and becomes a barrier.

K: I was told once by an Indian scholar that before people began to sculpt the head of a god, or whatever, they had to go into deep meditation. At the right moment they took up the hammer and the chisel.

DB: Then it came out of the emptiness. There is another point, you see. The Australian aborigines draw figures in the sand, so that they don't have permanency.

K: That is right.

DB: Perhaps thought could be looked at that way. You see, marble is too static, and remains for thousands of years. So although the original sculptor may have understood, the people who follow see it as a fixed form.

K: What relationship has all this to my daily life? In what way does it act through my actions, through my ordinary physical responses, to noise, to pain, various forms of disturbance? What relationship has the physical to that silent movement?

DB: Well, in so far as the mind is silent, the thought is orderly.

K: We are getting on to something. Would you say that the silent movement, with its unending newness, is total order of the universe?

DB: We could consider that the order of the universe emerges from this silence and emptiness.

K: So what is the relationship of this mind to the universe?

DB: The particular mind?

K: No; mind.

DB: Mind in general?

K: Mind. We went through the general and the particular, and beyond that there is the mind.

DB: Would you say that is universal?

K: I don't like to use the word universal.

DB: Universal in the sense of that which is beyond the particular. But perhaps that word is difficult.

K: Can we find another word? Not global. A mind that is beyond the particular?

DB: Well you could say it is the source, the essence. It has been called the absolute.

K: I don't want to use the word 'absolute', either.

DB: The absolute means literally that which is free of all limitations, of all dependence.

K: All right, if you agree that 'absolute' means freedom from all dependence and limitation.

DB: From all relationships.

K: Then we will use that word.

DB: It has unfortunate connotations.

K: Of course. But let's use it for the moment just for convenience in our dialogue. There is this absolute stillness, and in or from that stillness there is a movement, and that movement is everlastingly new. What is the relationship of that mind to the universe?

DB: To the universe of matter?

K: To the whole universe: matter, trees, nature, man, the heavens.

DB: That is an interesting question.

K: The universe is in order; whether it is destructive or constructive, it is still order.

DB: You see, the order has the character of being absolutely necessary; in a sense it cannot be otherwise. The order that we usually know is *not* absolutely necessary. It could be changed; it could depend on something else.

K: The eruption of a volcano is order.

DB: It is order of the whole universe.

K: Quite. Now in the universe there is order, and this mind which is still is completely in order.

DB: The deep mind, the absolute.

K: The absolute mind. So, is this mind the universe?

DB: In what sense is that the universe? We have to understand what it means to say that, you see.

K: It means, is there a division, or a barrier, between this absolute mind and the universe? Or are both the same?

DB: Both are the same.

K: That is what I want to get at.

DB: We have either duality of mind and matter, or they are both the same.

K: That's it. Is that presumptuous?

DB: Not necessarily. I mean that these are just two possibilities.

K: I want to be quite sure that we are not treading upon something which really needs a very subtle approach — which needs great care. You know what I mean?

DB: Yes. Let's go back to the body. We have said that the mind which is of the body — thought, feeling, desire, the general and the particular mind — is part of the material process.

K: Absolutely.

DB: And not different from the body.

K: That's right. All the reactions are material processes.

DB: And therefore what we usually call the mind is not different from what we call the body.

K: Quite.

DB: Now you are making this much greater in saying, consider the whole universe. And we ask if what we call the mind in the universe is different from what we call the universe itself?

K: That's right. You see why I feel that in our daily life there must be order, but not the order of thought.

DB: Well, thought is a limited order, it is relative.

K: That's it. So there must be an order that is . . .

DB: . . . free of limitation.

K: Yes. In our daily life we have to have that — which means no conflict, no contradiction whatsoever.

DB: Let's take the order of thought. When it is rational it is in order. But in contradiction the order of thought has broken down, it has reached its limit. Thought works until it reaches a contradiction, and that's the limit.

K: So if in my daily life there is complete order, in which there is no disturbance, what is the relationship of that order to the never ending order? Can that silent movement of order, of that extraordinary something, affect my daily life, when I have inward psychological order? You understand my question?

DB: Yes. We have said, for example, that the volcano is a manifestation of the whole order of the universe.

K: Absolutely. Or a tiger killing a deer.

DB: The question then is whether a human being in his ordinary life can be similar.

K: That's it. If not, I don't see what is the point of the other — the universal.

DB: Well, it has no point to the human being. You see, some people would say, who cares about the universe. All we care about is our own society, and what *we* are doing. But then that falls down, because it is full of contradiction.

K: Obviously. It is only thought which says that.
   So that universe, which is in total order, *does* affect my daily life.

DB: Yes. I think that scientists might ask how. You see, one might say, I understand that the universe is constituted of matter, and that the laws of matter affect our daily life. But it is not so clear how it affects the mind; and if there is this absolute mind which affects the daily life.

K: Ah! What is my daily life? Disorderly, and a series of reactions. Right?

DB: Well, it is mostly that.

K: And thought is always struggling to bring order within that. But when it does that, it is still disorder.

DB: Because thought is always limited by its own contradictions.

K: Of course. Thought is always creating disorder, because it is itself limited.

DB: As soon as it tries to go beyond the limit, that is disorderly.

K: Right. I have understood, I have gone into it, I have an insight into it, so I have a certain kind of order in my life. But that order is still limited. I recognize that, and I say that this existence is limited.

DB: Now some people would accept that, and say 'Why should you have more?'

K: I am not having more.

DB: But others might say, 'We would be happy if we could live in a material life, with real order.'

K: I say, let's do it! It must be done! But in the very doing of it, one has to realize it is limited.

DB: Yes, even the highest order that we can produce is limited.

K: And the mind realizes its limitation and says, let's go beyond it.

DB: Why? Some people would say, why not be happy within those limits, continually extending them, trying to discover new thoughts, new order? The artist will discover new forms of art, the scientists a new kind of science.

K: But all that is always limited.

DB: There is often the feeling that we can go this far, and accept that this is all that is possible.

K: You mean the feeling that we must accept the human condition?

DB: Well, people would say that man could do much better than he is doing.

K: Yes, but all this is still the human condition, a little reformed, a little better.

DB: Some people would say enormously reformed.

K: But it is still limited!

DB: Yes. Let's try to make clear what is wrong with the limitation.

K: In that limitation there is no freedom, only a limited freedom.

DB: Yes. So eventually we come to the boundary of our freedom. Something makes us react, through reaction we fall back into contradiction.

K: Yes, but what happens when I see that I am always moving within a certain area . . . ?

DB: Then I am under the control of the forces.

K: The mind inevitably rebels against that.

DB: That is an important point. You see the mind wants freedom. Right?

K: Obviously.

DB: It says that freedom is the highest value. So do we accept that, and see it just as a fact?

K: That is, I realize that within this limitation I am a prisoner.

DB: Some people get used to it and say, 'I accept it.'

K: I *won't* accept it! My mind says there must be freedom from prison. I am a prisoner, and the prison is very nice, very cultured and all the rest of it. But it is still limited, although it says, there must be freedom beyond all that.

DB: Which mind says this? Is it the particular mind of the human being?

K: Ah! Who says there must be freedom? Oh, that is very simple. The very pain, the very suffering demands that we go beyond.

DB: This particular mind, even though it accepts limitation, finds it painful.

K: Of course.

DB: And therefore this particular mind feels somehow that it is not right. But it can't avoid it. There seems to be a necessity of freedom.

K: Freedom is necessary, and any hindrance to freedom is retrogression. Right?

DB: That necessity is not an external necessity due to reaction.

K: Freedom is not a reaction.

DB: The necessity of freedom is not a reaction. Some people would say that having been in prison you reacted in this way.

K: So where are we? You see, this means there must be freedom from reaction, freedom from the limitation of thought, freedom from all the movement of time. We know that there must be complete freedom from all that, before we can really understand the empty mind, and the order of the universe, which is then the order of the mind. We are asking a tremendous lot. Are we willing to go that far?

DB: Well, you know that non-freedom has its attractions.

K: Of course, but I am not interested in these attractions.

DB: But you asked the question, are we willing to go that far? So it seems to suggest that there may be something attractive in this limitation.

K: Yes. I have found safety, security, pleasure in non-freedom. I realize that in pleasure or pain there is no freedom. The mind says, not as a reaction, that there must be freedom from all this. To come to that point and to let go without conflict, demands its own discipline, its own insight. That's why I said to those of us who have done a certain amount of investigation into all this, can one go as far as that? Or do the responses of the body — the responsibilities of daily action, for one's wife, children, and all that — prevent this sense of complete freedom? The monks, the saints, and the sannyasis have said, 'You must abandon the world.'

DB: We went into that.

K: Yes. That is another form of idiocy, although I'm sorry to put it like that. We have been through *all* that, so I refuse to enter again into it. Now I say are the universe and the mind that has emptied itself of all this, one?

DB: Are they one?

K: They are not separate, they are one.

DB: So you are saying that the material universe is like the body of the absolute mind.

K: Yes, all right.

DB: It may be a picturesque way of putting it!

K: We must be very careful also not to fall into the trap of thinking that the universal mind is always there.

DB: How would you put it then?

K: Man has said that God is always there; Brahman, or the highest principle, is always present, and all you have to do is to cleanse yourself, and arrive at that. This is also a very dangerous statement, because then you might say, there is the eternal in me.

DB: But I think that is projecting.

K: Of course!

DB: There is a logical difficulty in saying it is always there because 'always' implies time, and we are trying to discuss something that has nothing to do with time. So we can't place it as being here, there, now or again!

K: We have come to the point that there is this universal mind, and the human mind can be of that when there is freedom.

20 SEPTEMBER 1980, BROCKWOOD PARK, HAMPSHIRE

THIRTEEN

Can Personal Problems be Solved, and Fragmentation End?

KRISHNAMURTI: We have cultivated a mind that can solve almost any technological problem. But apparently human problems have never been solved. Human beings are drowned by their problems: the problems of communication, knowledge, of relationships, the problems of heaven and hell; the whole human existence, has become a vast, complex problem. And apparently throughout history it has been like this. In spite of his knowledge, in spite of his centuries of evolution, man has never been free of problems.

DAVID BOHM: Yes, of insoluble problems.

K: I question if human problems are insoluble.

DB: I mean, as they are put now.

K: As they are now, of course, these problems have become incredibly complex and insoluble. No politician, scientist, or philosopher is going to solve them, even through wars and so on! So why have human beings throughout the world not been able to resolve the daily problems of life? What are the things that prevent the complete solution of these problems? Is it that we have never turned our minds to it? Is it because we spend all our days, and probably half the night, in thinking about technological problems so that we have no time for the other?

DB: That is partly so. Many people feel that the other should take care of itself.

K: But why? I am asking in this dialogue whether it is possible to have no human problems at all — only technological problems, which can be solved. But human problems seem insoluble. Is it because of our education, our deep-rooted traditions, that we accept things as they are?

DB: Well, that is certainly part of it. These problems accumulate as civilization gets older, and people keep on accepting things

which make problems. For example, there are now far more
nations in the world than there used to be, and each one creates
new problems.

K: Of course.

DB: If you go back in time . . .

K: . . . a tribe becomes a nation . . .

DB: And then the group must fight its neighbour.

K: Men use this marvellous technology to kill each other. But we
are talking about problems of relationships, problems of lack of
freedom, this sense of constant uncertainty and fear, the struggle
to work for a livelihood for the rest of one's life. The whole thing
seems so extraordinarily wrong.

DB: I think people have lost sight of that. Generally speaking
they accept the situation in which they find themselves, and try to
make the best of it, trying to solve some small problems to alleviate
their circumstances. They wouldn't even look at this whole
situation seriously.

K: But the religious people have created a tremendous problem
for man.

DB: Yes. They are trying to solve problems too. I mean
everybody is caught up in his own little fragment, solving
whatever he thinks he can solve, but it all adds up to chaos.

K: To chaos and wars! That is what we are saying. We live in
chaos. But I want to find out if I can live without a single problem
for the rest of my life. Is that possible?

DB: Well, I wonder if we should even call these things problems,
you see. A problem would be something that is reasonably
solvable. If you put the problem of how to achieve a certain result,
then that presupposes that you can reasonably find a way to
do it technologically. But psychologically, the problem cannot be
looked at in that way; to propose a result you have to achieve, and
then find a way to do it.

K: What is the root of all this? What is the cause of all this
human chaos? I am trying to come to it from a different angle, to

discover whether there is an ending to problems. You see, personally, I refuse to have problems.

DB: Somebody might argue with you about that and say that maybe you are not challenged with something.

K: I was challenged the other day about something very, very serious. That is not a problem.

DB: Then it is a matter of clarification. Part of the difficulty is clarification of the language.

K: Clarification, not only of language, but of relationship and action. A problem arose the other day which involved lots of people, and a certain action had to be taken. But to me personally it was not a problem.

DB: We have to make it clear what you mean, because without an example, I don't know.

K: I mean by a problem something that has to be resolved, something you worry about; something you are questioning, and endlessly concerned with. Also doubts and uncertainties, and having to take some kind of action which you will regret at the end.

DB: Let's begin with the technical problem where the idea first arose. You have a challenge, something which needs to be done, and you say that is a problem.

K: Yes, that is generally called a problem.

DB: Now the word problem is based on the idea of putting forth something — a possible solution — and then trying to achieve it.

K: Or, I have a problem but I don't know how to deal with it.

DB: If you have a problem and you have no idea how to deal with it . . .

K: . . . then I go round asking people for advice, and getting more and more confused.

DB: This would already be a change from the simple idea of a technical problem, where you usually have some notion of what to do.

K: I wonder if we do? Surely technical problems are fairly simple.

DB: They often bring challenges requiring us to go very deeply and change our ideas. With a technical problem, we generally know what we have to do to solve it. For example, if there is lack of food, what we have to do is to find ways and means of producing more. But with a psychological problem, can we do the same?

K: That is the point. How do we deal with this thing?

DB: Well, what kind of problem shall we discuss?

K: Any problem which arises in human relationships.

DB: Let's say that people cannot agree; they fight each other constantly.

K: Yes, let's take that for a simple thing. It seems to be almost impossible for a group of people to think together, to have the same outlook and attitude. I don't mean copying each other, of course. But each person puts his opinion forward and is contradicted by another — which goes on all the time, everywhere.

DB: All right. So can we say that our problem is to work together, to think together?

K: Work together, think together, co-operate without the involvement of monetary issues.

DB: That is another question, whether people will work together if they are highly paid.

K: So how do we solve this problem? In a group, all of us are offering different opinions, and we don't meet each other at all. And it seems almost impossible to give up one's opinions.

DB: Yes, that is one of the difficulties, but I am not sure that you can regard it as a problem, and ask, what shall we do to give up opinions.

K: No, of course. But that is a fact. So observing that, and seeing the necessity that we should all come together, people still cannot give up their opinions, their ideas, their own experiences and conclusions.

DB: Often it may not seem to them like an opinion, but the truth.

K: Yes, they would call it fact. But what can man do about these divisions? We see the necessity of working together — not for some ideal, belief, some principle or some god. In various countries throughout the world, and even in the United Nations they are not working together.

DB: Some people might say that we not only have opinions, but self-interest. If two people have conflicting self-interests, there is no way, as long as they maintain their attachment to these, that they can work together. So how do we break into this?

K: If you point out to me that we must work together, and show me the importance of it, then I also see that it is important. But I can't do it!

DB: That's the point. It is not enough even to see that co-operation is important, and to have the intention of achieving this. With this inability there is a new factor coming in. Why is it that we cannot carry out our intentions?

K: One can give many reasons for that, but those causes and reasons and explanations don't solve the problem. We come back to the same thing — what will make a human mind change? We see that change is necessary, and yet are incapable or unwilling to change. What factor — what *new* factor — is necessary for this?

DB: Well, I feel it is the ability to observe deeply whatever it is that is holding the person and preventing him from changing.

K: So is the new factor attention?

DB: Yes, that is what I meant. But also, we have to consider what kind of attention.

K: First let's discuss what is attention.

DB: It may have many meanings to different people.

K: Of course, as usual, there are so many opinions!
   Where there is attention, there is no problem. Where there is inattention, every difficulty arises. Now without making attention itself into a problem, what do we mean by it? Can we understand it, not verbally, not intellectually, but deeply, in our blood? Obviously attention is not concentration. It is not an endeavour, an experience, a struggle to be attentive. You must show me the nature of attention, which is that when there is attention, there is no centre from which 'I' attend.

DB: Yes, but that is the difficult thing.

K: Don't let's make a problem of it.

DB: I mean that people have been trying this for a long time. I think that there is first of all some difficulty in understanding what is meant by attention, because of the content of thought itself. When a person is looking at it, he may think he is attending.

K: No, in that state of attention there is no thought.

DB: But how do you stop thought then? You see, while thinking is going on, there is an impression of attention — which is not attention. But one thinks, one supposes that one is paying attention.

K: When one supposes one is paying attention, that is not it.

DB: So how do we communicate the true meaning of attention?

K: Or would you say rather that to find out what is attention, we should discuss what is inattention?

DB: Yes.

K: And through negation come to the positive. When I am inattentive, what takes place? In my inattentiveness, I feel lonely, depressed, anxious, and so on.

DB: The mind begins to break up and go into confusion.

K: Fragmentation takes place. And in my lack of attention, I identify myself with many other things.

DB: Yes, and it may be pleasant — but it can be painful too.

K: I find, later on, that what was pleasing becomes pain.
So all that is a movement in which there is no attention. Right? Are we getting anywhere?

DB: I don't know.

K: I feel that attention is the real solution to all this — a mind which is really attentive, which has understood the nature of inattention and moves away from it!

DB: But first, what is the nature of inattention?

K: Indolence, negligence, self-concern, self-contradiction — all that is the nature of inattention.

DB: Yes. You see, a person who has self-concern may feel that he is attending but he is simply concerned with himself.

K: Yes. If there is self-contradiction in me, and I pay attention to it in order not to be self-contradictory, that is not attention.

DB: But can we make this clear, because ordinarily one might think that this *is* attention.

K: No, it is not. It is merely a process of thought, which says, 'I am this, I must not be that'.

DB: So you are saying that this attempt to become, is not attention.

K: Yes, that's right. Because the psychological becoming breeds inattention.

DB: Yes.

K: Isn't it very difficult, Sir, to be free of becoming? That is the root of it. To end becoming.

DB: Yes. There is no attention, and that is why these problems are there.

K: Yes, and when you point that out, the paying attention also becomes a problem.

DB: The difficulty is that the mind plays tricks, and in trying to deal with this, it does the very same thing again.

K: Of course. Can the mind, which is so full of knowledge, self-importance, self-contradiction, and all the rest of it, come to a point where it finds itself psychologically unable to move?

DB: There is nowhere for it to move.

K: What would I say to a person who has come to that point? I come to you. I am full of this confusion, anxiety, and sense of despair, not only for myself but for the world. I come to that point, and I want to break through it. So it becomes a problem to me.

DB: Then we are back; there is again an attempt to become, you see.

K: Yes. That is what I want to get at. So is that the root of all this? The desire to become?

DB: Well, it must be close to it.

K: So how do I look, without the movement of becoming, at this whole complex issue of myself?

DB: It seems that one hasn't looked at the whole. We did not look at the whole of becoming, when you said, 'How can I pay attention?' Part of it seemed to slip out, and became the observer. Right?

K: Psychological becoming has been the curse of all this. A poor man wants to be rich, and a rich man wants to be richer, it is all the time this movement of becoming, both outwardly and inwardly. And though it brings a great deal of pain and sometimes pleasure, this sense of becoming, fulfilling, achieving psychologically, has made my life into all that it is. Now I realize that, but I can't stop it.

DB: Why can't I stop it?

K: Let's go into that. Partly I am concerned in becoming because there is a reward at the end of it; also I am avoiding pain or punishment. And in that cycle I am caught. That is probably one of the reasons why the mind keeps on trying to become something. And the other perhaps is deep rooted anxiety or fear that if I don't become something, I am lost. I am uncertain and insecure, so the mind has accepted these illusions and says, I cannot end that process of becoming.

DB: But why doesn't the mind end it? Also we have to go into the question of being trapped by these illusions.

K: How do you convince me that I am caught in an illusion? You can't, unless I see it myself. I cannot see it because my illusion is so strong. That illusion has been nurtured, cultivated by religion, by the family, and so on. It is so deeply rooted that I refuse to let it go. That is what is taking place with a large number of people. They say, 'I want to do this but I cannot'. Now given that situation, what are they to do? Will explanations, logic and all the various contradictions, theories, help them? Obviously not.

DB: Because it all gets absorbed into the structure.

K: So what is the next thing?

DB: You see, if they say, 'I want to change', there is also the wish not to change.

K: Of course. The man who says, 'I want to change', has also at the back of his mind, 'Really, why should I change?' They go together.

DB: So we have a contradiction.

K: I have lived in this contradiction, I have accepted it.

DB: But why should I have accepted it?

K: Because it is a habit.

DB: But when the mind is healthy, it will not accept a contradiction.

K: But our mind isn't healthy. The mind is so diseased, so corrupt, so confused, that even though you point out all the dangers of this, it refuses to see them.

So how do we help a man who is caught in this to see clearly the danger of psychological becoming? Let's put it that way. Psychological becoming implies identification with a nation, a group, and all that business.

DB: Yes, holding to opinions.

K: Opinions and beliefs; I have had an experience, it gives me satisfaction, I am going to hold on to it. How do you help me to be free of all this? I hear your words — they seem quite right, but I can't move out of all that.

I wonder if there is another factor, another way of communication, which isn't based on words, knowledge, explanations and reward and punishment. Is there another way of communicating? You see, in that too there is danger. I am sure there is a way which is not verbal, analytical or logical, which doesn't mean lack of sanity.

DB: Perhaps there is.

K: My mind has always communicated with another with words, explanations and logic, or with suggestion. There must be another element which breaks through all that.

DB: It will break through the inability to listen.

K: Yes, the inability to listen, the inability to observe, to hear, and so on. There must be a different method. I have met several men who have been to a certain saint, and in his company they say all problems are resolved. But when they go back to their daily life, they are back in the old game.

DB: There was no intelligence in it, you see.

K: That is the danger. That man, that saint, being quiet and non-verbal in the presence of that saint they feel quiet, and think that their problems are resolved.

DB: But this is still from the outside.

K: Of course. It is like going to church. In an ancient church, or cathedral, you feel extraordinarily quiet. It is the atmosphere, the structure — you know; the very atmosphere makes you feel quiet.

DB: Yes, it communicates what is meant by quietness, non-verbally.

K: That is nothing. It is like incense!

DB: It is superficial.

K: Utterly superficial; like incense, it evaporates! So we push all that aside, and then what have we left? Not an outside agency, a god, or some saviour. What have I left? What is there that can be communicated, which will break through the wall that human beings have built for themselves?

   Is it love? That word has become corrupted, loaded, dirty. But cleansing that word, is love the factor that will break through this clever analytical approach? Is love the element that is lacking?

DB: Well, we have to discuss it; perhaps people are somewhat chary of that word.

K: I am chary beyond words!

DB: And, therefore, as people resist listening, they will resist love too.

K: That is why I said it is rather a risky word.

DB: We were saying the other day that love contains intelligence.

K: Of course.

DB: Which is care as well; we mean by love that energy which also contains intelligence and care; all that . . .

K: Now wait a minute: you have that quality and I am caught in my misery, anxiety, etc., and you are trying to penetrate with that intelligence this mass of darkness. How will you do it? Will that act? If not, we human beings are lost. You follow, Sir? Therefore we have invented Jesus, Buddha, Krishna — images which have become meaningless, superficial and nonsensical.

So what shall I do? I think that is the other factor. Attention, perception, intelligence and love — you bring all this to me, and I am incapable of receiving it. I say, 'It sounds nice; I feel it, but I can't hold it'. I can't hold it, because the moment I go outside this room, I am lost!

DB: That really is the problem.

K: Yes, that is the real problem. Is love something outside, as heaven — and all that stuff is outside. Is love something outside, which you bring to me, which you awaken in me, which you give me as a gift — or, in my darkness, illusion and suffering, is there that quality? Obviously not, there can't be.

DB: Then where is it?

K: That's just it. Love is not yours or mine; it is not personal, not something that belongs to anyone; love is not that.

DB: That is an important point. Similarly you were saying that isolation does not belong to any one person, although we tend to think of isolation as a personal problem.

K: Of course. It is common ground for all of us. Also, intelligence is not personal.

DB: But again, that goes contrary to the whole of our thinking, you see.

K: I know.

DB: Everybody says this person is intelligent, and that one is not. So this may be one of the barriers to the whole thing, that behind the ordinary everyday thought there is deeper thought of mankind, but we generally feel divided, and say these various qualities either belong to us, or they don't belong to us.

K: Quite. It is the fragmentary mind that invents all this.

DB: It has been invented, but we have picked it up verbally and non-verbally, by implication, from childhood. Therefore it pervades, it is the ground of our thoughts, of all our perceptions. So this has to be questioned.

K: We have questioned it — that grief is not my grief, grief is human, and so on.

DB: But how are people to see that, because a person who is experiencing grief feels that it is his personal grief?

K: I think it is partly because of our education, partly our society and traditions.

DB: But it is implicit in our whole way of thinking. Then we have to jump out of that, you see.

K: Yes. To jump out of that becomes a problem, and then what am I to do?

DB: Perhaps we can see that love is not personal.

K: Earth is not English earth, or French earth, earth is earth!

DB: I was thinking of an example in physics: if the scientist or chemist is studying an element such as sodium, he does not say it is his sodium, or that somebody else studies *his* sodium. And of course they compare notes, etc.

K: Quite. Sodium is sodium.

DB: Sodium is sodium, universally. So we have to say that love is love, universally.

K: Yes. But you see my mind refuses to see that, because I am so terribly personal, terribly concerned with 'me and my problems'. I refuse to let that go. When you say sodium is sodium, it is very simple; I can see that. But when you say to me that grief is common to all of us, this is difficult.

DB: This can't be done with time, but it took quite a while for mankind to realize that sodium is sodium, you see.

K: Is love something that is common to all of us?

DB: Well, in so far as it exists, it has to be common.

K: Of course.

DB: It may not exist, but if it does, it has to be common.

K: I am not sure it does not exist. Compassion is not 'I am compassionate'. Compassion is there, is something that is not 'me'.

DB: If we say compassion is the same as sodium, it is universal. Then every person's compassion is the same.

K: Compassion, love, and intelligence. You can't have compassion without intelligence.

DB: So we say intelligence is universal too!

K: Obviously.

DB: But we have methods of testing intelligence in particular people, you see.

K: Oh, no.

DB: But perhaps that is all part of the thing that is getting in the way?

K: Part of this divisive, fragmentary way of thinking.

DB: Well, there may be holistic thinking, although we are not in it yet.

K: Then holistic thinking is not thinking; it is some other factor.

DB: Some other factor that we haven't gone into yet.

K: If love is common to all of us, why am I blind to it?

DB: I think partly because the mind boggles; it just refuses to consider such a fantastic change of concept in a way of looking.

K: But you said just now that sodium is sodium.

DB: You see, we have a lot of evidence for that in all sorts of experiments, built up through a lot of work and experience. Now we can't do that with love. You can't go into a laboratory and prove that love is love.

K: Oh, no. Love isn't knowledge. Why does one's mind refuse to accept a very obvious factor? Is it the fear of letting go my old values, standards and opinions?

DB: I think it is probably something deeper. It is hard to pin down, but it isn't a simple thing, although what you suggest is a partial explanation.

K: That is a superficial explanation, I know. Is it the deep rooted anxiety, the longing to be totally secure?

DB: But that again is based on fragmentation.

K: Of course.

DB: If we accept that we are fragmented, we will inevitably want to be totally secure, because being fragmented we are always in danger.

K: Is that the root of it? This urge, this demand, this longing to be totally secure in our relationship with everything? To be certain?
   Of course, there is complete security only in nothingness!

DB: It is not the demand for security which is wrong, but the fragmentations. The fragment cannot possibly be secure.

K: That is right. Like each country trying to be secure, it is not secure.

DB: But complete security could be achieved if all the countries got together. The way you have put it sounds as if we should live eternally in insecurity, you see.

K: No, we have made that very clear.

DB: It makes sense to ask for security, but we are going about it the wrong way. How do we convey that love is universal, not personal, to a man who has lived completely in the narrow groove of personal achievement? It seems the first point is, will he question his narrow, 'unique' personality?

K: People question it; they see the logic of what we are discussing, yet, curiously, people who are very serious in these matters, have tried to find the wholeness of life through starvation, through torture — you know, every kind of way. But you can't apprehend or perceive or be the whole through torture. So what shall we do? Let's say I have a brother who refuses to see all this. And as I have great affection for him, I want him to move out of fragmentation. And I have tried to communicate with him verbally, and sometimes non-verbally, by a gesture or by a look; but all this is still from the outside. And perhaps that is the reason why he resists. Can I point out to my brother that in himself this flame can be awakened? It means he must listen to me, but my brother refuses to listen.

DB: It seems that there are some actions which are not possible. If a person is caught in a certain thought such as fragmentation, then he can't change it, because there are a lot of other thoughts behind it.

K: Of course.

DB: Thoughts he doesn't know. He is not actually free to take this action because of the whole structure of thought that holds him.

K: So how do I help — I use that word with great caution — my brother? What is the root of all this? We talk of his becoming aware — but all that is verbal; it can be explained in different ways — the cause, the effect, and all the rest of it. After I explain all this, he says, 'You have left me where I am'. And my intelligence, my affection, says 'I can't let him go'. Which means, am I putting pressure on him?

I am not using any kind of pressure, or reward; my responsibility is that I can't let another human being go. It is not the responsibility of duty and all that dreadful stuff. But it is the responsibility of intelligence to say all that to him. There is a tradition in India that one who is called the Maitreya Buddha took a vow that he would not become the ultimate Buddha until he had liberated other human beings too.

DB: Altogether?

K: Yes. You see, the tradition hasn't changed anything. How can one, if one has that intelligence, that compassion, that love, which is not of a country, a person, an ideal or a saviour, transmit that purity to another? By living with him, talking to him? You see it can all become mechanical.

DB: Would you say that this question has never really been solved?

K: I think so. But we must solve it, you follow? It has not been solved, but our intelligence says, solve it. No, I think intelligence doesn't say solve it; intelligence says these are the facts, and perhaps some will capture it.

DB: Well, it seems to me that there are really two factors: one is the preparation by reason to show that it all makes sense; and from there possibly some will capture it.

K: We have done that, Sir. The map has been laid out, and he has seen it very clearly; the conflicts, the misery, the confusion, the insecurity, the becoming. All that is extremely clear. But at the end of the chapter he is back at the beginning. Or perhaps he has a glimpse of it, and his craving to capture that glimpse and hold on to it becomes a memory. You follow? And all the nightmare begins!

   In showing him the map very clearly, can we also point out to him something much deeper than that, which is love? He is groping after all this. But the weight of body, brain, tradition — all that draws him back. So it is a constant battle — and I think the whole thing is so wrong.

DB: What is wrong?

K: The way we are living.

DB: Many people must see that by now.

K: We have asked whether man has taken a wrong turning, and entered into a valley where there is no escape. That can't be so; that is too depressing, too appalling.

DB: I think some people might object to that. The very fact that it is appalling does not make it untrue. I think you would have to give some stronger reason why you feel that to be untrue.

K: Oh, yes.

DB: Do you perceive in human nature some possibility of a real change?

K: Of course. Otherwise everything would be meaningless; we'd be monkeys, machines. You see, the faculty for radical change is attributed to some outside agency, and therefore we look to that, and get lost in that. If we don't look to anybody, and are completely free from dependence, then solitude is common to all of us. It is not an isolation. It is an obvious fact that when you see all this — the stupidity and unreality of fragmentation and division — you are naturally alone. That sense of aloneness is common, and not personal.

DB: Yes, but the ordinary sense of loneliness is personal in the sense that each person feels it is his own.

K: Loneliness is not solitude; it is not aloneness.

DB: I think all the fundamental things are universal, and therefore you are saying that when the mind goes deep, it comes into something universal.

K: That's right.

DB: Whether or not you call it absolute.

K: The problem is to make the mind go very, very deeply into itself.

DB: Yes. Now there is something that has occurred to me. When we start with a particular problem our mind is very shallow, then we go to something more general. The word 'general' has the same root as 'to generate'; the genus is the common generation . . .

K: To generate, of course.

DB: When we go to something more general, a depth is generated. But going on, still further, the general is still limited because it is thought.

K: Quite right. But to go profoundly, requires not only tremendous courage, but the sense of constantly pursuing the same stream.

DB: Well, that is not quite diligence; that is still too limited, right?

K: Yes, diligence is too limited. It goes with a religious mind in a sense that it is diligence in its action, its thoughts and so on, but it is still limited. If the mind can go from the particular to the general and from the general . . .

DB: . . . to the absolute, to the universal. But many people would say that is very abstract, and has nothing to do with daily life.

K: I know. Yet it is the most practical thing, and not an abstraction.

DB: In fact, it is the particular that is the abstraction.

K: Absolutely. The particular is the most dangerous.

DB: It is also the most abstract, because you only get to the particular by abstracting.

K: Of course, of course.

DB: I think that this may be part of the problem. People feel they want something that really affects us in daily life; they don't just want to get themselves lost in talking, therefore, they say, 'All these vapid generalities don't interest us'.

It is true that what we are discussing must work in daily life, but daily life does not contain the solution of its problems.

K: No. The daily life is the general and the particular.

DB: The human problems which arise in daily life cannot be solved there.

K: From the particular, it is necessary to move to the general; from the general to move still deeper, and there perhaps is the purity of what is called compassion, love and intelligence. But that means giving your mind, your heart, your whole being to this enquiry.

We have talked now for a long time, I think we have reached somewhere.

27 SEPTEMBER 1980, BROCKWOOD PARK, HAMPSHIRE